THE TIMES

# HOW YOU CAN
# GET THAT JOB!

**3RD EDITION**

## Rebecca Corfield

KOGAN
PAGE

First published in 1992
Reprinted 1994, 1995
Second edition 1999
Third edition 2003
Reprinted 2004

Kogan Page Limited
120 Pentonville Road
London N1 9JN
United Kingdom
www.kogan-page.co.uk

© Rebecca Corfield 1992, 2000, 2003

The views expressed in this book are those of the author and are not necessarily the same as those of Times Newspapers Ltd.

**British Library Cataloguing in Publication Data**

A CIP record for this book is available from the British Library.

ISBN 0 7494 3894 0

Typeset by Jean Cussons Typesetting, Diss, Norfolk
Printed and bound in Great Britain by Clays Ltd, St Ives plc

# Contents

# *Introduction*

## What are application forms?

Application forms are the most common method used by employers to recruit new staff. An application form is a document, filled in by all applicants for a job, that enables the employer to contrast the candidates. In this way a group can be selected to be invited in for interview. This process is often called shortlisting: a longer list of applicants is whittled down to a smaller number or a shorter list.

Application forms are normally printed pieces of paper that are sent and delivered by the post. They may be any length between two and eight pages. Increasingly they take the form of an electronic document that is completed and sent over the electronic mail (or e-mail) system. Organisations' Web sites can often contain the relevant application form when a vacancy arises, and candidates simply fill it in and return it through the Web site or by e-mail to the recruiter.

The whole purpose of completing an application form is to impress an employer enough to win yourself a place on the day the interviews take place. You should complete the form after thinking about the position, and should try to present your skills and experience in the light of what is required for the job.

Often the employer will send out details about the vacancy in the form of a job description or a person specification. A job description is a succinct summary of the main duties and responsibilities of the job, designed to convey to applicants and eventual job-holders the key areas of work. A person specification is an outline of the kind of person that the employer requires for the job. Often a person specification will include both essential attributes for the role and preferred ones.

# Example

Position: Finance Manager

## Job description

Main duties:
Running small, busy finance department
Organising payroll and monitoring income and expenditure
Managing team of three finance staff
Working closely with Director and providing regular reports for management
Liaising with other departments
Sorting out suppliers' or customers' financial queries

## Person specification

*Essential*
Experience of figure work
Excellent communication skills
Well-organised and able to work on own initiative
Computer skills

*Preferred*
Management or supervisory experience
Financial qualifications
Experience of manufacturing sector

## Letters of application

Sometimes an employer asks candidates for a particular vacancy to apply by letter, normally to accompany a curriculum vitae or CV. Such letters of application need to be direct, impressive and clear if they are to enable the applicant to get an interview. They should normally not be longer than two sides of A4 paper. Writing a letter with impact requires you to use good structure and punchy language, and provide comprehensive coverage of your skills and the contribution you can make to the organisation. It may take several goes to compose the best letter you can, but it could make the difference between success or failure. Chapter 6 contains hints and tips on effective letter writing.

# The importance of application forms

Do you find that you complete application forms as well as you can, but you are not invited to interview? Something about the way in which you make your application must be holding you back.

Applying for jobs is a complicated procedure. It is also a skill that we are never formally taught and we are rarely able to see examples of other people's efforts. Yet the application form or letter that you send in pursuit of a vacancy is normally the only deciding factor in whether or not you are asked to an interview.

It is vital in a competitive job market to present yourself in the best light. This is not easy but there are ways to improve your techniques so that your application stands out from the rest. All job-seekers can benefit from having well thought-out and presented application forms. In addition to applying for jobs or for promotion at work, there are often forms to complete before starting college courses or government training schemes.

Even if you are in the job of your choice, knowing how to fill in application forms properly is still important. The days of a 'job for life' are long gone and now we are all likely to change jobs many times. This means that everyone needs to be able to impress an employer in writing in order to be offered an interview.

# How to get the most out of this book

This book takes you through the whole process, starting from the beginning when the application form lands on your doormat through to delivering the completed document to the employer. It establishes a system for job applications that enables you to take more control of the operation. Good candidates are not born lucky; they put time, effort and enthusiasm into the task in order to succeed. This book will be especially useful to the first-time job-seeker who wants to know how to stand a good chance of being selected for interview but, even if you have completed many forms before and are a veteran interviewee, it is easy to become sloppy about your paperwork. You may not have applied for a new job for some time and might want to check that you are approaching the task in the best way.

By reading this book, you will be able to check that you are making the most of your skills, experience and personality on

every form that you send off. You will come over more effectively to employers and this will enable you to get on more
interview shortlists. When you are faced with a blank application form, or need to write a letter applying for work, it can be
difficult to know where to start, especially if you are not sure
what the employer is really looking for. This book takes you
through the various stages and shows you what applying for
jobs is all about.

Chapter 1 looks at the changing world of work and explains
what is involved in the process of applying for jobs. It discusses
the application form as one method of finding a job and points
out the most important aspects of its completion. Chapter 2
analyses exactly what employers are looking for when they
want to take on staff. Also included is an explanation of what
leads to failure with application forms. To improve your
chances of success you need to pin-point the most important
aspects of the job from the employers' point of view. Spending
time thinking about the job on offer and researching the organisation concerned can provide all the answers that you need. In
addition, approaching the task feeling as good as you can helps
your chances of success. In Chapter 3 a typical application
form is examined and each section is studied in turn to explain
what sort of information should be included. The way that
forms look is as important as the information they contain and
aspects of presentation are covered in Chapter 4. This chapter
covers every aspect of presenting yourself on paper, from using
computers to choices of pen and paper. Some common problems are covered too.

Chapter 5 runs through examples of difficult or unusual
questions together with suggested answers. A list of dos and
don'ts for completing forms is included. Chapter 6 shows how
letters of application can be written effectively, detailing what
to include and how to express yourself. Sometimes you might
want to send a letter with your application form, and how to
do this is shown here. The concluding chapter, Chapter 7,
contains five topical case studies, each showing a common

situation concerning application forms. The chapter goes on to give a checklist of steps for approaching the tricky task of filling in job applications and takes you through the process involved. At the end of the book you will find pointers on using the Internet in your job search, as well as a list of other sources of help.

# The Process of Applying for Jobs

## The changing world of work

Even as recently as 30 years ago, most jobs would be filled with a direct approach to an employer followed by an interview. Now the situation has changed. In the past, you might have stayed in the same position for much of your working life; now you are likely to change jobs frequently – the average is every seven years. This may be because you want to move about or it may be because you are forced to make the change, perhaps due to redundancy or some other reason. As more part-time and temporary vacancies are advertised you are likely to be completing application forms more in the future too. There will be many people interested in any one vacancy and the employer has to have a way of deciding which few people to interview for each job. An application process is a convenient way for an employer to compare and contrast different candidates.

This forces you to learn about how to present yourself well on paper. Even if very little writing work comes into the job you want, you have to get over the hurdle of the application form in order to get an interview. The ability to present your views on paper is an invaluable skill in any field, and goes a long way to impressing an employer. Most people dread having to project themselves and find it doubly hard to do so through a written form. This is because it is difficult to know how you will come across to other people. You do not have the employer sitting opposite you when he or she reads your form to see the reaction to what you have said about yourself. This means you have to spend extra time making sure that every application you complete is positive, well written and clear about what you have to offer.

This sort of advertisement appears regularly in newspapers, inviting interested candidates to contact the company if they want to know more about the job on offer.

---

### ADMINISTRATIVE ASSISTANT

Flexible person wanted to help run busy solicitor's office. Clerical experience preferred but training given. Full-time, £24,500 pa.

Application and job description from:

**S & J Matthews**
**Solicitors**
**150 The Grange**
**Kelmsworth**
**Northants**
**Tel: 000–000–0000**

Closing date 22/9/2003

---

*Job advertisement*

If, after seeing an advertisement like this, you are interested in applying for the job, contact the employer and ask for an application form and further details. Enclose a stamped addressed envelope for the company to return the application form to you. When you write or phone, if it is not clear from the advertisement, ask if there is a job description available. Make sure that you keep the original details of the advertisement in case you are not sent any additional information.

# Why do we have application forms?

It is worth spending a little time analysing exactly what the application procedure is all about. When employers advertise for new staff they know that they will attract a wide variety of candidates. They want to find out about each applicant in order to assess which one will be the most suitable for the job on offer.

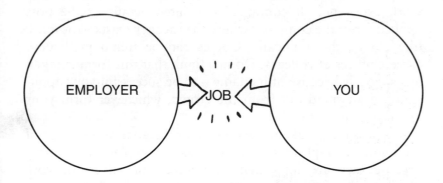

In the first instance, candidates are asked to write to the employer, either by sending in their curriculum vitae (CV) with a covering letter, or by filling in an application form.

Both these approaches will be covered in this book. Application forms are used because employers need some method of comparing the abilities, experience and personalities of those people who apply. A form which asks each person exactly the same questions means that quick comparisons can be made between different candidates. By comparing like with like, employers can be confident that they have made the best choice of whom to interview.

The types of forms used by employers vary considerably. They can be any length – from one short page to seven or more pages – and they are usually printed. Some examples are included on pages 96–109. The exact number and type of questions depends on the nature and level of the job concerned. Some smaller organisations have the same form for every job in the company. This can make it difficult to fill in for jobs that require fuller answers. The questions have been set for every job from the Chief Executive to the cleaner!

Students are sometimes asked by employers to complete a special type of form called the Standard Application Form. This is a general form which can be used to apply to different companies where candidates are not expected to have much work experience. It contains no printed details of the post applied for or the company where the vacancy exists – these are filled in by the applicant. Copies can be found in student careers offices at colleges. Do not think that this form is taken less seriously because of its name – to be successful your application must stand out from the crowd, whichever form your application is written in.

It is possible to take more control of the application stage of job-hunting. Employers only ask you to complete their forms because they are interested in finding out all about you. However, it is difficult to represent yourself properly when you are relying on just a few sheets of paper. The challenge in applying for jobs is to find ways to make yourself sound interesting enough for the employer to want to invite you for an interview.

Sometimes able and well-qualified candidates are put off applying for suitable jobs because they are daunted by the prospect of filling in a complicated form for a particular job. Pages of questions which require thought and careful preparation can appear confusing and difficult at first reading. It is unusual to find a new job without having to fill in some kind of paperwork, so the more forms you complete, the better your chances of success – as long as you do them well.

Making applications for jobs is a serious matter. Each one needs time and care in order to complete it properly. However, even the most difficult form can be tackled successfully given the proper techniques. It makes sense to establish a system to ensure that you give yourself every possible chance to get the job of your choice. As with any difficult task, splitting the work up into smaller less daunting parts can be helpful. The next few chapters explain in detail how to organise yourself to be successful. In addition to using good techniques, you need to be in the right frame of mind to 'sell yourself' effectively on paper. To establish yourself in the mind of the employer as someone worth interviewing, you must believe it yourself!

The only way to get a job is to keep making applications to different employers. Assuming that you fill in your forms to a high standard and are applying for suitable jobs, you are bound to succeed eventually. It is important to evaluate your progress and learn from your experience of job-hunting, so that you can continually improve your applications. Applying for a series of jobs at the same time not only increases your chances of success but also ensures that you do not build up your hopes around any one job in particular. You will not be so disappointed at rejection for a certain position if you know that you have other applications in the pipe-line, any of which could be successful.

However, there is no point in making applications if you are not really serious about the vacancy. Do not just go through the motions of applying. If you do, your efforts will be half-hearted and a rejection is inevitable. Choose to apply for jobs that would motivate you, and put all your efforts into presenting yourself to the best of your ability.

## Points to remember

- The application part of the job search process is vital if you are to get an interview. It is not just a formality. Your success depends upon how well you do it.
- Employers need to know all about you in order to decide if they would like to meet you in an interview.
- By doing some careful planning you can choose the best way to describe yourself on an application form.
- Many application forms are now submitted on-line and those submitted in hard copy form may be scanned by the employer, so legibility is now more important than ever.

## Dos and don'ts

Do:

- start each application afresh with energy and enthusiasm;
- prepare to spend considerable time and effort on every application you make;
- allow yourself plenty of time to complete and check the form.

Don't:

- keep all your eggs in one basket – keep applying for different jobs that interest you;
- make flippant applications – if you are going to do it, do it properly;
- lose track of your applications – be organised about your paperwork.

# What are Employers Looking For?

## How jobs are advertised

Jobs can be advertised in a variety of ways. One of the most common ways of hearing about vacancies is through newspapers, although other methods involve advertisements in Job Centres or local shops; word of mouth; local radio stations; and professional or specialist journals. If you have access to a computer and the Internet, there are increasing numbers of job advertisements on-line. Larger employers will maintain details of any vacancy for their organisation on their Web site, and application forms for current jobs can often be downloaded direct without having to contact the employer first. Recruitment organisations and employment agencies also publish job vacancies on the Internet. Their Web sites often contain hundreds of jobs that are updated very regularly. Such Web sites often include a facility for searching for specific types or levels of vacancy, to help you pinpoint relevant jobs more quickly. You can also elect to be informed of suitable new vacancies on these sites as and when they are posted.

Certain local and national newspapers carry advertisements

for jobs in every issue, often with different types of work being advertised on different days. The interested job-seeker is asked to apply in writing with a CV or send off for an application form. Papers also have their own Web sites which carry vacancy information. See 'Using the Internet' on page 110 for details. Companies will often send out information about their products or services, as well as a description of the job vacancy concerned.

However, many jobs are never advertised at all. Research suggests that approximately 70 per cent of all jobs are filled without being advertised. Sometimes employers wait for potential applicants to contact them. Chapter 6 tells you more about the way to write impressive letters of application to send with your CV or general enquiries to ask employers if they have vacancies. Some employers tell their existing staff that there is a vacancy and invite applications by word of mouth.

Application forms are one method of giving an employer information about your suitability as a candidate for a particular post. An example is shown on page 96. The form may be any length but is usually between two and four pages. Normally printed in black ink on white paper, it contains a series of questions designed to encourage the applicant to give certain information about him or herself. Many of the questions will be followed by a box in which you can write your answer.

# Why applications fail

Let us consider first what can put an employer off calling you to interview. These are the top 10 reasons selectors give for rejecting written applications:

- not answering the questions set on the form fully or properly, eg too short answers, not doing justice to their skills and abilities;

- too much waffle, however interesting, giving too long answers, using ten words when five would do;
- using pretentious language instead of normal speech;
- assuming the selectors understand jargon and the key tasks in the applicant's present role when they have not been properly explained;
- leaving unclear exactly how they satisfy each point on the person specification;
- being half-hearted and not selling themselves on the page, not showing any real enthusiasm for the job;
- not showing that they have fully considered all aspects of the vacancy, eg indicating a dislike of paperwork when it is obvious that this forms a large part of the job in question;
- not giving concrete examples, just claiming that they can do the job;
- completing the form too hastily and making errors of spelling, grammar or layout;
- being vague or unclear, eg 'I was involved with...': this could mean anything from managing the project to making the tea.

Reading this list, you may think it is a difficult task to get your application forms in just the right state to impress an employer. The good news is that all of these mistakes that could lose you the chance of an interview can be avoided through adequate preparation about your selling points, careful attention to the form and allowing plenty of time for its completion.

# The need to 'sell yourself'

We have seen that application forms need to contain positive statements about yourself. It is not enough to give a list of what you have done and the skills that you have acquired. You need to see application forms principally as a method for you to 'sell yourself' to an employer. In today's competitive job market, there will be many hopeful applicants for every job. Only the most distinctive application forms will stand out enough for the senders to be picked for interview.

It used to be the case that anyone who could satisfy the minimum conditions laid down in a job description would automatically be shortlisted for interview. Although it is true to say that applicants will not be picked for interview without establishing that they fulfil the basic conditions, because of the increasing number of candidates it is now essential to put forward a much stronger application.

Out of 100 applicants for a position, half may be weeded out as unsuitable at an early stage because they fail to demonstrate that they meet the essential requirements. However, this still leaves a large number of applicants who might be able to do the job. The employer will be looking closely for any clues that an applicant should be taken forward to the next stage. This means convincing the employer that there would be some extra benefit or added value in including you in the shortlist for interview. More applicants mean that the criteria for each job are raised and employers can afford to be more choosy. In other words, you have to try harder in order to succeed.

All employers are keen to know what skills you have learnt in previous jobs that will be useful in the future. These 'transferable skills' are those that will be helpful across different roles, eg communication skills, computer ability or being a good team player. You need to prove that you are the most 'employable' candidate available.

Companies are looking for the best candidates for their vacancies and your application needs to shout out loud that you are one of those candidates. But judgement about who is the best candidate will vary according to the job on offer. That is why it is essential to get inside the head of the employer to examine what exactly he or she is looking for with each vacancy. One way to impress people is to show enthusiasm. You are in competition with many other keen applicants who are all trying to impress. A genuine interest and excitement about the work involved in the job shows even through a written page.

Consider the following two examples in answer to the question:

## 'Why do you think that you are suitable for this position?'

(working as an accounts assistant)

*John's answer:* 'I am quite good with numbers. My last job involved calculating and checking figures and I tried to be accurate. I took my GCSE in mathematics and did well at school in this subject.'

*Michelle's answer:* 'Working with numbers is a challenge. I take a great pride in being accurate and did especially well in the mathematics GCSE course at school. I very much enjoyed my last job which involved a great deal of figure work, calculating totals and checking figures for the department I worked in. I am keen to make my career in this area.'

You can see how Michelle's reply abounds with energy and enthusiasm for the work. She achieves this effect by choosing bolder and more definite language, letting the words depict her keen attitude to this kind of work. She creates the feeling that she would come in to work each Monday morning beaming with delight at the prospect of a new week!

# How to approach the task

Application forms are split up into different sections and each is concerned with a different subject. Their sole purpose is to find out about the candidates and those candidates whose forms contain the most impressive information will be invited for interview. However, it is extremely difficult to put yourself across effectively on paper alone. To create a good impression you need to give the employer as *full details* as possible about yourself. Applicants who do not write much are doing themselves out of their best chance of getting the job.

The most important point to remember is that *neatness* gives you a great advantage in the hunt for the job of your choice. It has been shown that employers will reject perfectly well-qualified, suitable candidates if they send in badly presented applications. There are two reasons for this. The first is that how a document looks creates a strong first impression. The only information that the employer has to go on to decide whether to pick you for interview is your application form. He or she will make judgements about your attitude to work and other people on the strength of the way you have filled in your form. The second reason is that it is hard to take in information from the printed page, let alone the handwritten one, and neat writing is much easier to follow than messy scrawl. Your application forms need to be as well presented as possible to stand out from the rest without being distracting. Chapter 4 covers how to ensure all your application forms are well presented.

Sometimes it is tempting to send in your CV instead of spending time filling in the same information on the form. However, if the employer wanted your CV, he or she would have asked for it. To send it as a substitute for filling in an application form tells the employer that you cannot really be bothered to spend time applying for the job. It also shows that you are not prepared to follow instructions. Of course, if the company asks to see your CV in addition to your application form that is quite a different matter. In this case the CV should be short and concise. More than two or three pages will be too long to hold the reader's interest. But when you are answering the questions on the application form you need to make your answers long enough to interest the employer without being long-winded.

Beware too of simply copying information from one job application on to the next form you have to complete. Each and every new application form needs to be treated as though you are starting anew. Of course, the factual details about your background will be the same but the way you present yourself should be specifically tailored to the job in question.

The well-written response that drags on is liable to bore the reader just as much as the poorly written one. To make sure that your answers are written in a coherent way, you must *organise* your thoughts in advance. Chapter 3 gives more information about thinking through and planning your answers systematically before you start to write anything. This ensures that you do not duplicate, muddle up or miss out any information.

## Positive mental attitude

Employers are looking for more than just the right kind of answers in the boxes on an application form. They are also looking for people who consider themselves to be winners and successful operators in their field. This may seem a hard attitude to strike if you have just been made redundant, have left your last job under a cloud or have been unemployed for some time. However you need to boost up your feelings about the contribution you could make, for the very good reason that unless you believe it yourself, you will be unable to convince anyone else of the fact.

There are certain attitudes in job-seekers that will definitely put an employer off. In order of significance they are:

1. Disruptive, wanting to cause trouble.
2. Cynicism about employers' motives.
3. Bitterness about previous experiences.
4. Lazy, just wanting to do the minimum possible.
5. Lack of confidence in own abilities.

If you feel you may exhibit any of the above you will have to work doubly hard to retrain yourself to come across differently. While it may be totally justifiable to feel aggrieved at the treatment you had in previous work situations, it is not helpful to extend that feeling into the next job. You need to spend some time generating positive feelings of optimism and hope for what could occur.

How do you make your outlook positive? You will need to use every good thing in your life to help you. Ask those who love you best to tell you what they value most about you. Read old letters or references to see what people find impressive about you. Stick to your normal routines when embarking on a job search programme, as making applications involves uncertainty and risk, and a regular living pattern will help to balance this.

If there are some activities that you love such as having foam-filled baths, taking weekend breaks or having breakfast in bed, then do them. If you find the company of certain people stimulating, then invite them round. Physical exercise can get you fitter whilst providing you with a regular burst of positive energy. Working for other people on a voluntary basis can get you more externally rather than internally focused.

Consider all the times that you have succeeded at something, and try to recreate both the energy you put into making the effort and the feeling you experienced afterwards. You need to concentrate your mind on approaching the task of applying for this job in a focused and determined manner in order to do your best.

## Points to remember

- Employers only have the information on the application form to make their decisions about which candidates to invite for interview.
- Selling yourself depends on strong statements, enthusiastic language and clarity about what you have to offer.

- The frame of mind in which you start making applications can make all the difference.
- Some companies now vet applicants by telephone before sending out application forms.

## Dos and don'ts

Do:

- give priority to making yourself feel good, so that you can convey an impression of confidence to an employer;
- think about jobs from the employers' point of view, and consider what will have the most impact on them;
- approach every application sincerely: if it is worth completing it is worth completing properly.

Don't:

- worry about being boastful – all the other applicants will be highlighting their strong points;
- waste time applying for jobs that do not motivate you – it will show in your lacklustre answers;
- take short cuts to filling in the form, you need to give it time and energy for an application to be successful.

# 3

# *What to Put in Your Application*

The secret of filling in application forms is to take the task seriously. If you are not prepared to devote a certain amount of time to this activity, you are probably not that interested in the job itself. Getting the job you want is an important business and demands the same care and time that you would devote to a college essay or a school work project.

If you are not keen enough to allow sufficient time for completing the form, the employer will realise this and you will not get the job. My rule of thumb is that you should aim to spend at least one day of preparation for each page of the application form. Of course, not all sections of the form will take as long as each other, and you will not be spending the whole of each day poring over pieces of paper, but this is a rough guide to how much input each job application requires. You may feel that this is a lot of exertion for each job, but think about what you have to gain. The salary (or wages) that you would earn just in the first year amounts to thousands of pounds, which is a lot of money, and is surely worth the investment of some effort. So, given that this is a task which you agree should be taken seriously, what is the right way to complete it? The best way to approach filling in the form is to split the task up into easy stages.

# The planning stage

## The task

When the application form arrives on your doormat, take a photocopy of it. Libraries, job clubs and local shops now have photocopying equipment, although you may have to pay for your copies. If you do not have access to a photocopier, write out the questions by hand on to scrap paper, then put the original form away for safe keeping. You will now only be working on the copy that you have made until you are confident that you have sorted out exactly what to say for each of your answers. In this way you will keep the original top copy in perfect condition until the time comes to complete it.

The secret of a good application is to allow yourself plenty of time before the closing date – preferably a day for each page of the form. Impressive writing cannot be done when you are feeling pressurised and rushed. You need to have an appropriate location in which to undertake this work. Find a quiet place where you can concentrate on the task in hand. You will need a clear desk or table with enough space to spread out all the relevant pieces of paper and a good light by which to read, write or type. Try to make sure that you will not be disturbed, and switch the television off! Now is the time to concentrate on this task alone, in order to immerse yourself in all the details of the job. Have a current copy of your CV to hand to give you the facts and dates about your career history. Your favourite type of music played quietly in the background may help to put you in the right mood. Focus on what you are doing and try to blank out any other concerns you have or distractions around you.

## The vacancy

Before you start, re-read the details of the job carefully from any information you have been sent or have discovered yourself. Take a note of or underline the main requirements/ skills/qualifications asked for. If you do not have any of these requirements it is unlikely that you will be asked to an interview. However, if you do have different skills and experience or alternative qualifications to those specified and feel that you could do the job, go ahead and apply. Many people get good jobs by taking chances like this, on the basis that they do not have anything to lose. However, the onus is on you to state clearly what you *are* offering as an alternative to the qualifications or experience asked for and why your background makes you suitable for the position.

A certain amount of time must be spent thinking through the nature of the vacancy for which you are applying. Each job is different and requires different qualities, skills and experience. Moreover, every organisation has a different feeling or culture and is looking for people who will fit in. The big, bustling, high-street department store will be looking for candidates who can work happily in that environment, while a small country firm of solicitors will require a different type of staff.

## Yourself

At the planning stage you also need to spend time thinking in some depth about who you are and what you have to offer relative to the company and its requirements. You should prepare a good CV which gives details about your qualifications and experience to date. This can be used as an *aide-mémoire*, or memory-jogger, to fill in certain parts of your application form and also as a confidence booster at a time when you need to be thinking about your achievements. A properly written CV can give an overview of your strengths and skills and help you to present yourself well when applying for jobs. It is vital to link your skills, knowledge and experience to the duties involved in the job.

Now is the time to inflate your own self-confidence as much as possible. On most application forms there is a question about your personal qualities and how these will enable you to contribute to the post on offer. The following exercise will help you to prepare your answer to this type of question. Most of us could reel off a long list of our faults but we find our strengths more difficult to pinpoint. For this exercise, you will need to dispense with the feeling that you are boasting, take a deep breath and describe yourself in the best possible light.

## Exercise: Your good points

Most people find this exercise tricky because we are not used to applauding ourselves in this way, which is exactly why it is such a useful thing to do. Perhaps you can remember being complimented on some facet of your character or behaviour, either in person or in a school or college report. You may have had favourable comments made about you in an appraisal or performance review from a previous workplace. What was said then? How would your best friend describe your good points to someone who had not met you before?

In the space overleaf make a list of 10 of your good qualities. Each point should comprise one word or short phrase and relate to your behaviour. Here are some examples. You may find some which apply to you and could be included in your list:

| | |
|---|---|
| flexible | articulate |
| calm | organised |
| punctual | tactful |
| sensible | alert |
| quick to learn | reliable |
| practical | cooperative |
| polite | loyal |
| lively | responsible |
| dedicated | versatile |
| creative | good at keeping to deadlines |
| confident | able to work under pressure |

approachable

assertive

accurate

perceptive

consistent

innovative

careful

strong

direct

adaptable

bright

thoughtful

imaginative

dependable

friendly

outgoing

serious-minded

quick

buoyant

hardworking

capable

thorough

able to work alone

good team member

committed

good at managing others

competent

humorous

decisive

enthusiastic

cautious

patient

dynamic

methodical

self-motivated

sensitive

honest

cohesive

Everybody's list will be different according to the personality of the writer. Write your description here, choosing the 10 words or phrases that you feel best depict your character strengths:

1

2

3

4

5

6

7

8

9

10

This type of list is useful for two reasons. First, it provides you with the raw material to answer questions about your strengths or personal qualities and second, it enables you to see your good points laid out on paper as a boost to your confidence. If you are an appropriate candidate for a job vacancy, you of all people need to feel confident that you have the personality and experience to do the job well. Unless you believe it, you will not be able to convey that impression to anyone who reads your application form. So spend some time thinking about yourself, what you have been praised for in the past and the advantages to an employer in taking you on.

## Your experience

You also need to plan which aspects of your past to mention. Large gaps in your career history will be noticed, but this still leaves you with a certain amount of leeway as to how you tell the story of your experience to date. Generally, information provided by you must be relevant to the job (and so will change with the different positions that you apply for) and should have purpose. Otherwise, the good points that you include will be lost in general trivia that do not add anything to your form. The way that information is put over has an impact on the way it is received. It will never be relevant to divulge that you failed a flute exam at school, but it may be worth saying that you studied the instrument when you were younger.

Active verbs or power words can be useful in describing your achievements to date. The following list may prove helpful when you are writing about your experience. There are many other words which may apply to you but here are some examples:

coordinating

computing

caring

persuading

establishing

serving

travelling

diagnosing

assessing

analysing

copying

negotiating

managing

training

teaching

memorising

deciding

checking

compiling

carrying

helping

mending

problem-solving

evaluating

writing

reading

cleaning

driving

drawing

liaising

inputting

growing

advising

recruiting

performing

leading

developing

filing

sorting

typing

loading

handling

communicating

researching

selling

inventing

recording

stocking

delivering

playing

working

making

monitoring

interpreting

selecting

translating

supervising

planning

enabling

changing

If you are applying for a certain type of work, the organisation concerned will want to see evidence of your direct experience in this field.

A national organisation which recruits volunteers to work abroad always asks candidates if they have done any voluntary work before. Applicants often answer 'No' when it should be obvious that this will not be sufficient. In such a case the employer needs to be convinced that you are capable of sustaining an interest in volunteering. Even if the experience was some time ago it is worth mentioning. Candidates for this type of vacancy with no voluntary experience should join a scheme and get involved in some voluntary work immediately so that they can fill in the form adequately. If they have not picked up some experience of this key area of the job, their application is likely to be rejected at an early stage.

## Analysing the job

Deciding what skills and abilities are required is not a matter of guesswork but of using common sense. Consider the following job advertisement:

---

### TREETOPS NURSERY

Small estate-based nursery needs a part-time childcare assistant to help with general duties. 17.5 hours per week. Personality more important than experience. Training given.

For application form write to:

**Treetops Nursery**
Garrick Estate,
Tonbridge, Kent
or phone 000-0000.

---

Even with these few details we can work out what sort of person would be suitable for the job. We know that the employer is interested in three main things: experience, skills and personality (that is, what you have done, what you know and the kind of person you are). Let us consider each of these in turn.

*Experience*
Although the advertisement says that training will be given and experience is not necessary, many applicants will be able to provide some experience so it would be helpful to offer some evidence of your ability to do this type of work. Perhaps you have brought up children of your own, helped out in other childcare schemes or been a babysitter or a childminder in the past. Even if none of these examples would be classed as a 'proper' job, this kind of experience would indicate your ability in this area.

*Skills*
In this sort of work the right person will be punctual and good at time management. Budgeting and organising skills will come in handy as well as attention to detail and the ability to schedule events. Knowledge of home economics would be an asset. An awareness of health and safety is important when working with young children and even confidence with shopping would be a selling point. Being able to handle paperwork competently would be a definite advantage.

*Personality*
In terms of personality, we have to think about the sort of person who can work with children. He or she needs to be well balanced, reliable and organised, with a tolerant and happy disposition. Someone who is observant and patient, who enjoys playing with and entertaining children of all ages and has an understanding of the problems and concerns affecting children would be ideal. The right person should enjoy teaching and

What the employer is looking for

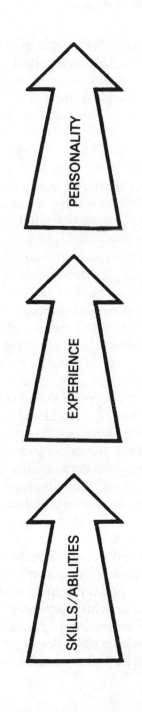

SKILLS/ABILITIES

EXPERIENCE

PERSONALITY

communicating with other people and using his or her imagination. A good childcare worker finds it easy to care for children and is able to create a disciplined environment with the right mixture of fun and control.

These points are the basic requirements for anybody who wants to work with children. To apply for this job, an applicant needs to show that he or she has had this type of experience, together with the skills and personality required by quoting examples from previous jobs. Any job can be analysed in this way, even with little information to start with. You need to use your imagination, your common sense and research into what is involved in the job.

## Finding out more

If you are not sure what the company is looking for, you need to do some detective work. Research into the products or services sold, the numbers of offices or outlets and staff, the main markets and the style of the organisation, is never wasted. It enables you to feel confident about your knowledge of the business, and you can impress the interviewer by talking up in the interview about your research on the company.

You can try to talk to people who work at the firm by ringing up and asking for information; you can look up facts about different organisations in libraries or ask people who work in similar jobs for their impressions of the company or the type of work that you are interested in. Companies often advertise their products or services in magazines, local and national newspapers and on the Internet.

Most medium and large organisations have a Web site from which you can research almost anything you need to know about the company. Often the site will show how the organisation describes itself, clearly outlining its vision and mission statement. It may well include profiles of key staff together with a brief history of, and background to, the development of the company. You may find that the way the information is written and displayed tells you more about the kind of organisation and how it sees itself than does the content of the site. It may be trying to portray a young, dynamic and creative image, or instead be labouring its pedigree, long traditions and solid trading background.

These impressions are very important, as they can tell you whether or not you would fit well into the organisation. Do the values that the company express seem important to you? Is this the kind of organisation that you want to be associated with? Could you see yourself working here? Try to pinpoint exactly what impresses you, so that you can reflect this in your application later on. Not just having done research, but being able to show you have done so, can enhance your chances of being called for interview.

If you need to locate businesses of a certain type or a particular company, you could use a search engine: a Web site that can help you track down the kind of information you need. www.google.co.uk is a useful Web address that can effectively link you to a host of other sites. Researching around the organisation that interests you is always worth doing. You may well discover relevant facts about the sector or area of business that could be mentioned in an interview to show your understanding of the kind of work. Make sure that you establish both the good and bad points of the job, so you are confident that you have a realistic picture of both its opportunities and its difficulties.

You may be applying for a different job or a promotion in the organisation in which you already work. Do not make any assumptions about being known or about your reputation if you are applying as an internal candidate. Even if you have worked in the same team for years and your supervisor is doing the recruitment for the new position, you must treat the form as though no-one reading your details will have ever heard of you before. You may be working in the department where the new job is located but your suitability for the post will be judged solely on the form you submit and only on the information it contains.

# The preparation stage
## Taking care

First, read carefully through the copy that you have made of your form. Then work your way through it, considering how you are going to approach filling it in. Never start writing on the original form straight away, even if it appears easy to complete. Errors and corrections do not enhance any form. If you do not read through a form thoroughly before you start to complete it, you can often make unnecessary mistakes. Some forms have duplicate questions that mean you may only need to complete half the form depending on your situation. If you rush to start writing, you may find that you have filled in a section that does not apply to you.

That sort of error can leave you looking at a messed-up form and feeling demoralised when you badly need more confidence, not less. Sometimes there will be similar sounding questions which require quite different answers, and it is worth checking what the form is looking for in each answer. If you rush to write things down too quickly it can mean that you miss the subtleties of the question, duplicate your answers, and perhaps miss the point of a particular question entirely. If you are not totally confident about your spelling, make sure you use a dictionary. There is no excuse for misspelled words. Line up a friend, relative or work colleague who is willing to check your work later on. Use black ink or ball-point pen and not pencils, crayons or felt-tipped pens.

Normally, you need to make your answers fit the space provided, and fill up that space completely. However, if the form suggests that you may like to continue on a separate sheet of paper if you do not have enough room for your answer, you should do so. The employer is saying that he or she expects a longer answer than there is room for on the page. Everybody else who applies for the job will use an extra sheet and, to do your answer justice, you need to do the same.

Take all questions on the form at face value and never assume that the employer is trying to catch you out. The reason you have been sent an application form is to find out more about you and see if you are a suitable candidate for interview. However, there may well be searching or difficult questions which will require you to think hard about the job and work out what kind of special contribution you think you could bring to it. Trick questions or those deliberately designed to confuse or fool you do not appear on application forms.

# Completing the different sections

Application forms usually come in two distinct parts, sometimes characterised as the 'easy' bit and the 'difficult' bit. The easy bit is the first section that asks for details about you, the applicant. This normally includes personal details, academic qualifications, work experience, interests and references. This part of the form is often considered simpler to complete because the information is factual to a large extent, and you just need to fill in the boxes with straightforward information about yourself.

Although the information required may be relatively easy to fill in, do be sure that you read the form carefully so that you know what is wanted. If the employer asks for specific information, or requests that you give the information in a particular way, and you do not do this, you may lose the chance of the job. For instance in the employment history section, if the small print on the form asks for your most recent job first and you give the list in date order with your first job at the top, you might stand out as the only candidate who was unable to follow the written instructions on the form, which is bound to create a poor impression. Although this is not a terrible crime in itself, if an employer has 60 applications for one post, any reason to reduce the pile by one will be seized upon.

If you are adept at using computers and can access the form electronically, you may decide to complete it on screen. It can take a lot of time to space it correctly and arrange it properly, so do not feel you have to do this if it would not be easy for you. Be aware too that some employers like to see your handwriting, so will not mind at all if you complete this part of the form by hand.

Now let us take each of these sections in turn to see what kind of answer the employer is looking for from each one. The following sections usually appear on every application form.

*Personal details*

The first section of the form is concerned with your personal details. These questions ask your name, address and other facts. You will not have any opportunity to 'sell yourself' here. You will normally be asked to give your first and second names in full and your address. You must give your telephone numbers for home and work (if applicable). Always include a personal e-mail address if you have one, but think carefully before giving a work e-mail address unless you are confident that it is private enough.

If you are not on the telephone you should find a friend or relative who can take messages for you, should the employer decide to phone you. Make sure that you ask permission before giving out anybody else's number and do not give your current work number if it will cause trouble should a potential employer decide to ring you up.

You will be asked for your date of birth, and sometimes your age as well. You will have to state your nationality and sometimes answer further questions about your eligibility to work in this country. These questions are not being asked just out of curiosity. The employer needs to check that you are allowed to work here if offered the job. You may be asked for a description of your general state of health. An application for a Civil Service position may ask many more detailed questions about your background, including details about your parents, whether you have ever had any other nationality, your place of birth and so on.

You may be asked where you saw the advertisement for the post. This is to tell the employer how effective the company's recruitment advertising is. It is helpful if you can give precise details.

Some people are tempted to include a recent head and shoulders photograph with their form. Unless this is specifically requested because physical appearance is relevant to the job, you should not do it. If your application is the only one with a photograph attached it will look very odd.

*Academic qualifications*
You need to give the names and addresses of places where you have studied. The employer will want to know particulars of qualifications obtained (classes, divisions, etc) and the names of courses or subjects studied, if appropriate. If you have recently left school or college you will be expected to make more of this experience by giving full information about subjects taken or projects worked on.

Do not send in copies or originals of your exam certificates unless you are specifically asked to. A list of your qualifications will suffice at this stage.

*Work experience*
This section of the form is where you expand on your previous work experience. The aim is not just to produce a list of all the jobs that you have ever had, but rather to explain what skills and abilities you have to offer a new employer. Most space on the form will normally be allocated to your current or last job. This is on the understanding that the most recent job will probably be the one which afforded you most responsibility. You will often be asked for a brief outline of the duties performed, and sometimes the salary or wage that you were paid. You do not need to send in copies of payslips with your form, though.

If you are employed at present you may be asked for details of the notice that you are required to give.

Most forms ask that previous jobs should be put in a logical order (usually, the most recent first) and you will be asked to give details of the posts held, the names and addresses of the employers, and the dates concerned. Sometimes you will be asked why you left each job and the salary at that time. In this case it is important that you give only *positive* reasons for leaving previous jobs. If you complain about former companies, colleagues or employers it will look as if you are a difficult person who is capable of running down the recruiting company in the future.

*Interests*

There may be a section where you are asked to outline your leisure interests and activities. You will need to show that you are a well-rounded person with a variety of hobbies or interests outside work. It helps to have some sporting or active interests and others which use your mind or involve creativity. A selection of different types of activities will show this and as many as eight pastimes could be mentioned. It does not matter if you have not done all the things on your list recently, as long as you would be happy to discuss them in an interview. This means that you must know about or be interested in every item that you write down here.

*Referees*

You may be asked for particulars of two (or sometimes three) people to whom reference may be made about your suitability for the work concerned and your character. These references are not normally taken up unless you are picked for the job, but you must always ask permission before you put anyone's name down as a referee. You will need a name, title, address and telephone number for each person. An e-mail address is also helpful.

Do not put 'available at interview' if asked for referees, as it will appear that you have something to hide. You must arrange for suitable referees to be available when you are completing any form.

The rest of any application form contains the questions that require more attention, with challenging subjects that need effort, creativity and attention to detail for their completion.

*Equal opportunities*
You will sometimes find a question about equal opportunities for jobs with large corporations, voluntary organisations, local authorities or charities. Any organisation which works with the general public may be interested in your attitude to the issues raised by this subject. This kind of question is more difficult to answer. If you find a question such as 'What does equal opportunities mean to you?' on a form, it requires some thought. Like most difficult questions, there is no precise, correct answer, but the employer will want to know that you take the subject seriously. You need to illustrate this in your response by defining the phrase and saying how it is important to the job. One of the best ways is by using other words to explain it. You could say: 'Equal opportunities mean everyone getting the same chances in employment and access to services.'

In some cases the employer will go further and ask: 'How would you put equal opportunities into practice in this job?' Your answer should contain references to the way that the services in question need to be accessible to all the people being served and what measures could be taken for ensuring that this happens. Treating people fairly applies to staff as well as clients, though, and you should also mention that you are keen to play your part as a sympathetic and supportive team member within the organisation itself. If you can mention an example of the way you have worked with clients or colleagues that you feel illustrates your fair treatment of other people, this will count in your favour.

*Statement by candidate*

This section can appear in various guises. A typical form of words is: 'Give any other information which you consider will be helpful in support of your application.' Some versions split this question into several smaller questions such as, 'What experience do you have that makes you suitable?', 'Describe the education and training you have received and why it is relevant to this post' and so on. This will normally be the biggest blank space on the form; it is the section generally left to last and it will require the most work. Do not see completing this answer as a problem to be dreaded. Instead, view it as a gift – a way of summing up why you deserve to be called for an interview and a chance to really impress the employer. It is often better to answer this question on a computer if you have access to one, as the answer normally represents a large block of words. You may find that the form provides a limited amount of space and invites you to 'Use additional sheets if necessary'. This generally means that you are expected to take up more space than has been provided on the form, and the employer assumes that to do the question justice you will need more paper. Use the space on the form to write 'Please see attached sheet/s' and start your answer on extra paper that you can fix firmly to the finished form. Always include your name and contact details on each and every additional sheet that you use in case they get separated from your application form.

The most important point to remember is that the answer that you give should tell the employer what you think you can contribute to the organisation, not why you want to work there. So you must find ways of stressing what you have to offer. Each candidate will be anxious to get the job because of the benefits that come with it, such as the wages, job security etc. What the employer wants to hear is how you can add to the work being done by the organisation. Chapter 5 provides guidelines and examples of how to answer such questions.

You need to present your strong points which match the job requirements. Start by studying any information you have been sent by the employer. The most common documents sent out to accompany an application form are the job description and a person specification. These will have been written for the specific job you are applying for, so that applicants can be clear what is required and how they can best fulfil the requirements. If these documents are provided you must show you meet the criteria as written down, or you will automatically not be shortlisted. Most employers start the filtering process by ticking off the elements of the job description and person specification that the applicant demonstrates. Often this level of screening applicants is performed by the personnel office or human resources department. The person doing this may not have any specialist knowledge of the job role concerned, so will only take into account how far you show you match the written job requirements.

It may sound a boring process but you need to deliberately work your way through each item listed and draft a short paragraph to say, 'I am (whatever they have asked for), as demonstrated by (your relevant example)' to ensure you do not miss any of the points out. Do not assume that the employer will understand what you mean unless you explain fully. Saying you have five years computing experience may not get you a tick against a job description which requires you to be fluent at using spreadsheets and database applications. You need to state clearly, 'I have used Excel spreadsheet package in my work for the last three years and am confident at entering and managing data to track orders and oversee customer activity.'

Your answer must:

- demonstrate that you match each part of the person specification;
- give examples to show that you have experience of every component of the job description;
- highlight skills and experience that may not be directly asked for, but that you feel are relevant, explaining why you think so;

● describe your personality and why you think you would be good in the job and what you would add to the team.

From studying the advertisement and information provided about the job, you should be able to highlight these requirements and ensure that, as far as possible, you satisfy them. Remember that you can describe your work experience in different ways, depending on the exact nature of the position concerned. For example, in one case you may emphasise the experience you obtained in handling people and achieving things. In another case, you may need to emphasise the amount of work you did, analysing and interpreting data, preparing reports and contributing to the development of new ideas, policies and procedures. Detail about the precise way in which you worked is not required. What are relevant to the employer are the transferable skills involved in each case, ie those skills that will be equally useful in the job you are applying for.

Employers are interested in three main areas:

● your skills;
● your experience;
● your personality.

You may be asked about your career ambitions. You should convey enthusiasm about the job and imply that you will want to progress within the company without seeming to have way-out or aggressive ambitions.

## Mind the gap!

We all have aspects of our history which need some explaining. It may involve a time when you were not working for some reason, or a job which ended more abruptly than you would have liked. Whether it is a period of unemployment, some time in prison or detention, or being sacked from a position, you will need to explain, in the most positive way, what happened to you during that time.

## Monitoring form

Some employers will send you another form to complete with your application form. It asks for details of your ethnic origin and if you have any disabilities. Often the form will explain what it will be used for: 'The information contained in this form will help us to monitor the percentage of applicants that we employ from different ethnic groups. On receipt of your application it is filed separately and will not be considered in conjunction with your application'. Sometimes applicants worry that this information may prejudice the employer against them, but this is not the case. The employer is just trying to find out how fair their recruitment policies are and the information will help them to put their equal opportunities into practice.

*Acknowledgement card*
You may find a card has been enclosed with your application form. This is for you to complete with your name and address so that the employer can send it back to you when he or she receives your application. Normally, only large companies are this well organised, so return it to them with your application. You will know that your form has arrived safely when the card is posted back to you.

## *Points to remember*

- Always start by working to any information provided about the job, especially the job description and person specification. Unless you can prove that you meet all the points they contain, you will not be invited for interview.
- Establishing a clear idea of the kind of organisation the vacancy is with will enable you to think more easily about the job and how you would fit in. Study any information about the company, especially its Web site and publicity materials.

● Pay just as much attention to the 'easy' bits of the form as to the more 'difficult' parts. Errors or omissions anywhere may limit your chances of success.

## Dos and don'ts

Do:

● write the form out in rough first;
● use a computer to type your written statement;
● give examples where possible as evidence of your claims.

Don't:

● attempt to type the whole form unless you are a confident, skilled and accurate typist;
● tell lies on your form – you can be sacked if you are subsequently found out;
● leave the more difficult questions so late that you do not have time to complete them impressively.

# *Presentation*

The way in which you complete your form is regarded by employers as important. The vital lesson to learn from this book is: *the way that your form looks is as crucial as what you have written on it.* When your application lands on an employer's desk, he or she will give it a three-second glance to gain a first impression before deciding whether it is worth studying more closely. The most comprehensive and well thought-out forms can be ruined because of lack of time and trouble taken in filling them in. No matter how good a candidate you are in theory, if your form does not look neat and easy to read, you are unlikely to be considered for the job.

To illustrate the importance of this point, study the two examples overleaf. They are simple application forms which contain the same information but are very different in appearance.

I have seen many untidy and messy forms like Janet's which have been carelessly completed with too little time dedicated to the task. Some employers would simply discard her form without even reading it. It is difficult to tell which way she has answered some of the questions and, because she did not draft the form in rough first, her spacing is haphazard and the form is difficult to read.

No doubt Janet thought that companies would be so interested in the content of her form that the way it looked was less important than what it contained. Unfortunately, as you can see, bad presentation, however nice the writing, makes it a trial to read, particularly when there is a pile of 50 other forms to be read.

---

**APPLICATION FORM**

Confidential                    *(please use black ink)*                    When completed, return to:

Application for ~telumu,           Ref: EB/ C24 J
appointment of: Assistant

SURNAME ___STACEY___           OTHER NAMES ___Janet___
*(IN BLOCK LETTERS)* Mr./Mrs/Miss        *(IN BLOCK LETTERS)*

Maiden name ___—___  Marital status ___Single___  Ages of children, if any ___—___
*(if appropriate)*
Address ___23 Bryan House Rotherhithe___
___Street London SE16 1HB___

Telephone No. 0000-000-0000
Age ___43 Yrs.___  Date of Birth ___15.4.59___

Are you a registered disabled person? YES/NO   if yes, state Reg. No. and nature of disability

---

**EDUCATION, TRAINING AND QUALIFICATIONS**

| Schools, Colleges and Universities attended since age 11 *(with dates)* | Qualifications and Certificates obtained *(give dates, grades, subjects)* |
|---|---|
| Camp Hill School Kings Heath BIRMINGHAM B14 1971 to 1977 | O'Levels — 9 subjects including ENGLISH LITERATURE & MATHEMATICS ALL JUNE 1975 A' LEVELS - ECONOMICS GRADE B, ENGLISH GRADE E. BOTH JUNE 1977 |
| KINGSTON POLYTECHNIC KINGSTON-UPON-THAMES, SURREY 1977 to 1980 | BA (HONOURS) SOCIAL SCIENCE specialising in Development Studies. Class II June 1980 |

Where did you see the post for which you are applying advertised? EVENING GAZETTE

P.T.O.

**PREVIOUS APPOINTMENTS TO DATE**
*(the most recent first)*

| Employer's name and address *(and nature of business)* | From | To | Position held and duties | Reason for leaving |
|---|---|---|---|---|
| Trusty Insurance Co Unit 7 The Park Twickenham Surrey TW9 0PZ (Insurance Company) | 1989 | Date | Administrative Assistant Filing, answering the phone, writing and posting letters, dealing with the public and keeping the diary, taking minutes of meetings | I would like to work for the Civil Service to help the public |
| Langdale Motor Company Bermondsey Road London SE19 1TG | 1981 | 1989 | General hand Keeping the office diary and answering the phone. Generally helping out & taking messages etc. | Offered a position with more variety in an office environment. |
| Different restaurants Temporary work | 1980 | 1981 | Various catering jobs in London | To go to a permanent position |

**NAMES AND ADDRESSES OF TWO REFEREES**
*(Please give your last employer as a reference if possible)*

(1) Ms D McKenna (owner) Trusty Insurance Co Unit 7 The Park Twickenham Surrey TW9 0PZ

(2) Mr B Neate (Accountant) 407 The Glades Suffolk Road Mitchley Bedfordshire BD3 1LL

May your referees be contacted for a reference if you are selected for interview?   YES/NO

Supplementary questions for posts involving driving or use of a vehicle.
Do you hold a current driving licence?      YES/NO   If so for what types of vehicle?

Do you own or have the use of a vehicle?      YES/NO   If so what type?

Signature _Janet Stacey_      Date _3rd May '02_

## APPLICATION FORM

| Confidential | (please use black ink) | When completed, return to: |
|---|---|---|

Application for appointment of: ADMINISTRATIVE ASSISTANT     Ref: OB/C24J

SURNAME STACEY     OTHER NAMES CECILIA
(IN BLOCK LETTERS) Mr/Mrs/Miss     (IN BLOCK LETTERS)

Maiden name N/A     Marital status SINGLE     Ages of children, if any N/A
(if appropriate)

Address 23 BRYAN HOUSE, ROTHERHITHE STREET, LONDON. SE16 1HB.

Telephone No. 0000-000-0000

Age 43 YEARS     Date of Birth 15.4.59

Are you a registered disabled person? YES/NO     if yes, state Reg. No. and nature of disability

N/A

**EDUCATION, TRAINING AND QUALIFICATIONS**

| Schools, Colleges and Universities attended since age 11 (with dates) | Qualifications and Certificates obtained (give dates, grades, subjects) |
|---|---|
| CAMP HILL SCHOOL KINGS HEATH BIRMINGHAM B14 1971 TO 1977 | O' LEVELS: 9 SUBJECTS INCLUDING ENGLISH LITERATURE AND MATHEMATICS. ALL JUNE 1975 |
| | A' LEVELS: ECONOMICS GRADE B } JUNE 1977 ENGLISH GRADE E } |
| KINGSTON POLYTECHNIC KINGSTON-UPON-THAMES SURREY 1977 TO 1980 | B.A. (HONOURS) SOCIAL SCIENCE SPECIALISING IN DEVELOPMENT STUDIES. CLASS II. JUNE 1980 |

Where did you see the post for which you are applying advertised? EVENING GAZETTE     P.T.O.

**PREVIOUS APPOINTMENTS TO DATE**
*(the most recent first)*

| Employer's name and address *(and nature of business)* | From | To | Position held and duties | Reason for leaving |
|---|---|---|---|---|
| TRUSTY INSURANCE COMPANY, UNIT 7, THE PARK TWICKENHAM SURREY TW9 0PZ (INSURANCE COMPANY) | 1989 | DATE | ADMINISTRATIVE ASSISTANT: FILING, ANSWERING THE PHONE, WRITING AND POSTING LETTERS DEALING WITH THE PUBLIC AND KEEPING THE DIARY, TAKING MINUTES OF MEETINGS. | I WOULD LIKE TO WORK FOR THE CIVIL SERVICE TO HELP THE PUBLIC. |
| LANGDHLE MOTOR COMPANY BERMONDSEY ROAD LONDON SE1 9TG | 1981 | 1989 | GENERAL HAND: KEEPING THE OFFICE AREA TIDY AND ANSWERING THE PHONE. GENERALLY HELPING OUT BY TAKING MESSAGES ETC. | OFFERED A POSITION WITH MORE VARIETY IN AN OFFICE ENVIRONMENT. |
| DIFFERENT RESTAURANTS (TEMPORARY WORK) | 1980 | 1981 | VARIOUS CATERING JOBS IN LONDON | TO GO TO A PERMANENT POSITION. |

**NAMES AND ADDRESSES OF TWO REFEREES**
*(Please give your last employer as a reference if possible)*

(1) MS D. MCKENNA
(OWNER)
TRUSTY INSURANCE CO.
UNIT 7, THE PARK
TWICKENHAM
SURREY TW9 0PZ.

(2) MR B. NEATE
(ACCOUNTANT)
407 THE GLADES
SUFFOLK ROAD
MITCHLEY
BEDFORDSHIRE RD3 1LL

May your referees be contacted for a reference if you are selected for interview?   YES/~~NO~~

Supplementary questions for posts involving driving or use of a vehicle.

Do you hold a current driving licence?   YES/NO   If so for what types of vehicle?

Do you own or have the use of a vehicle?   ~~YES~~/NO   If so what type?

Signature  Cecilia Stacey.          Date  3rd May '02

If there was a choice to be made between Janet and Cecilia, which would you pick?

Be aware that particular jobs mean that employers may look for different signs of your potential from your application. With any job concerned with administration, writing or paperwork of any kind the employer will be ruthless about the way that your answers are written. When I recruit people to work with job-seekers, I expect all the applicants to submit beautifully prepared CVs. Similarly, employers offering work concerned with art and design matters will notice the details of your presentation. You should pay particular attention to the way that you space and lay out your writing for this type of work.

The key to a well-presented document is planning and preparation. Although it takes time, you should never write up an application form straight away without composing a rough draft first. This means that you can make your mistakes on the rough version and, when you are happy with your answers, copy them on to your neat, final version. Use lined paper under the final version so that you can keep the lines straight and always use a ruler to underline, end a section or delete information. If you do make an error, cross it through neatly with a single line or use correction fluid to make an invisible repair. Little details like this can mean the difference between success and failure.

## Spelling

Bad spelling is inexcusable on application forms and will normally mean that your application will not be read right through, even if it is for a job that does not require a great deal of written expertise. If you know that your spelling and grammatical skills are weak, make sure that you check all the difficult words by using a dictionary and allow extra time to get a good speller to check the form thoroughly for you.

If you are applying for a job which involves writing and know you are weak in this area, you may want to get some help to improve your spelling and grammar, for example at an evening class. It is never too late to learn and you will find local colleges are full of people just like you.

## Writing or typing?

Unless you are a skilled typist, it is best to handwrite your form. Application forms are difficult to type because of the need to fit your answers into the spaces provided. Unless you are an expert at the fiddly job of lining up type and calculating how much room your answer will take, your efforts at typing will look much messier than a neatly written form. If you are handwriting your form, consider capital letters for bullet points or lists, as they are much easier to read than lower-case script. Note the difference between Cecilia's capital letters and Janet's lower-case writing in the examples on the previous pages. If you do decide to type the application, complete one version in rough first to make sure that you have calculated the spacing correctly. Words running off the page, uneven lines and cramped sentences will detract from your answers.

## Using computers

Modern computers and scanners have transformed the way application forms can be completed for those who have access to such equipment and who are confident and skilled at using it. If you scan a form, make sure you keep to the original amount of space provided as far as possible, tempting though it is to stretch the form out to fit your needs. Remember that the reason the employer is using an application form is to be able to compare candidates easily.

If you are using a computer without a scanner, copy out the form exactly as it is on the paper and try to use the most similar typeface or font that you can find, so that it does not look as though you have altered the form. Once you have all the headings in place you can type in your answers and print out the form. Many people use a combination of handwriting and typing to complete their forms. They will fill in by hand all the factual questions about their personal details and employment experience and use a computer to type out the rest. This means that the longer questions such as 'Why are you applying for this post?' will have 'Please see attached sheet' on the form, together with the completed answer typed out on a plain piece of paper inserted into the final document. If you include extra pages in this way make sure that they are very clearly labelled as belonging to you, in case they get separated from the main form.

Increasingly employers put their application forms on their organisation's Web sites so that they can be downloaded direct from the Internet. This means you can access forms immediately without having to request them and then wait for them to be posted to you. They can often be sent back to the company electronically too, just by you completing them on screen and redirecting them back. In this case all the form will be typed and there will be no option to handwrite sections of it unless you decide to print it off, complete it on paper and then post it back to the employer.

# Improving your writing

If you know that your handwriting is untidy, you must allow extra time for this part of the process. Most writing can be improved by using capital (or upper-case) letters all the way through the form. It is difficult to write in straight lines in an empty box. Put lined paper underneath the form so that the lines show through and act as a guide. Alternatively, you can pencil fine lines on the form itself, as long as you remember to rub them out carefully before you send off the finished application. A black pen should always be used as blue ink does not show up well if the form is photocopied (for other people in the company). Make sure that the pen you use does not blotch and smudge on the paper by buying or borrowing a good quality ink pen.

# Style

Writing the form out neatly is important, but so are ordering the contents logically and making the key points stand out. It is difficult to absorb information from the printed page and trying to conjure up a picture of an individual from answers on a form is even more problematic. Yet that is what the employer is trying to do when he or she reads your form. Therefore it makes sense to think through in some detail what you want to convey. The best answers are not written straight on to the page but considered and arranged before the act of writing them down.

Some applicants think that they should change their style of writing to make it more formal and try to use long and complicated words that they would not normally use. Far from impressing the reader, this can sound stilted and old-fashioned, which is probably not the way that you want it to appear. You can be confident that if you write as though you are talking directly to the reader, you will sound fine. The important thing to concentrate on, as far as style is concerned, is that your writing is easy to read and understand.

You cannot assume that the reader knows what you are talking about unless you have explained clearly and simply. You should aim to tread the fine line between giving enough detail and ensuring that you are concise in your explanations.

You will see from the example on page 48 that the use of note form or bullet points can help there.

## Layout

Think about the layout of the writing on the page when you are filling in your first rough copy. Each piece of information should be enclosed in its own border of white space to keep it separate from the next item. The contents of your form can be made to look more attractive and eye-catching with the judicious use of underlining, so make your qualifications and job titles stand out from the rest of the information presented. The example on page 48 illustrates this and bullet points can also be used to show the key elements.

## Additional sheets of paper

If the application form invites you to 'continue on a separate sheet of paper if necessary', it is best to do so. The employer is indicating that he or she thinks it likely that you will need more space than that provided to give an adequate answer. Most of the other applicants will be using the extra space allowed, so your answer will look brief in comparison if you do not do the same.

It makes sense to keep a supply of stationery if you are applying for jobs. Good quality envelopes and paper make a difference to the way your application looks and mean that you are never without the 'tools' to apply for a job that comes up. However, do ensure that you always use the same colour paper as the original form (usually white) if you are sending in extra pages of your own.

Do not use any coloured paper that is darker than ivory or cream, as it will not photocopy clearly and your answers may be obscured if copies need to be made.

# Some common problems

## 'My writing is too big to fit into the space provided.'

The advantage in completing your form on a rough copy first is that you can spend time arranging your answers to fit the form. You must scale down your writing to ensure that you have room to answer adequately, even if you need several attempts to get it small enough. It is preferable to use different-sized writing from your normal style, to ensure that you put enough detail in your answers.

## 'My experience doesn't seem to tally with what the job requires.'

It may be that the job is not suitable for you, in which case you need to do more thinking about the sort of work you are looking for. It is difficult to get a job when you really have no relevant qualifications, experience or attributes. If you are trying to break into a new career you will need to prove that, although different, your previous experience has given you the type of skill that will be transferable enough to enable you to make a contribution to the company concerned.

For instance if you have managed projects before but the position is looking for someone who has had experience of managing staff, you will need to be able to show that the skills that you have developed are similar to the ones they are looking for. You surely have to plan the projects you are responsible for now, and timetable a schedule of work; communicating the key aims and point of your projects may be a priority; if a team works with you, you may have to liaise between all the different parties; and thorough project management will involve monitoring progress, evaluation and review. This list represents skills that are essential to managing a team of people, even if you cannot claim to have run your own team so far.

## 'I have only just left college and don't have any work experience yet.'

The challenge here is to minimise your weakness – that you have not yet worked – and maximise your experiences at college. It need not be formal work experience that counts here. You could offer experience of voluntary work or part-time jobs as substitutes. Helping out in a local project can show that you have commitment to a certain type of work and that you have picked up the skills demanded in the job you are applying for. Use this time when you are making applications to start some kind of part-time or voluntary work so that you will not have the same problem in the future.

It is extremely rare for employers to take someone on with no work experience at all. Recognise the fact that you need to build up a bank of working skills to provide evidence that you will be valuable in a paid job. Even if all your experience is in a voluntary role, this could make the difference between you and another candidate. Voluntary work could also provide you with good references and contacts, and confidence in your own abilities.

## 'I didn't do well at school and don't have any qualifications to put down.'

You need not worry about this as long as you have something else to offer the employer. Your work experience can show that you learn quickly, apply yourself and can take a disciplined environment. If you feel you could now benefit from a second chance at education, then enrolling on a local college course will always look impressive to future employers. Not everyone is best suited to taking exams at 16, and you may find that returning to learning at a later stage enables you to have a much more successful experience with studying.

## 'I just can't get excited about the job. I keep putting off the task of filling in the form.'

It may be necessary to consider whether this job is really the one for you. If you have spent some time thinking about the form and how your skills, personality and experience are suitable for it, and yet still cannot work up any enthusiasm for the task, perhaps it is not worth bothering. Many application forms are thrown away without being completed because the applicants find the closing date has arrived and they have made no progress with the form.

On the other hand, we all find filling in application forms hard work, and this often makes the task seem daunting. Most people underestimate the time needed to do the job properly. It may be that you need to devote more creativity and energy to the task. You really have to summon up all your confidence and pride in order to sell yourself to the employer and be ready to take at least as many days as there are pages in the form to do it justice. Shut yourself away from all distractions, concentrate on the form and tell yourself how good you'll feel when it is done and in the postbox. Don't let the chance of a good job pass you by for the lack of some hard work.

## 'Some of my answers only fill in a few lines when the space provided is huge.'

This probably means that you have not spent enough time preparing your answers. The space given usually corresponds to the size of the answer that you are expected to give. All the other candidates will be making sure that they use all the available space, and your form needs to match. Imagine your form being considered along with the others. If yours obviously has shorter answers, it may be rejected without being read. You will need to start planning your answers again, this time going into much more detail about what you have achieved, what you know and what you can contribute. Think through all aspects of the job and pick the brains of friends and relatives about what other relevant information you could include. Do not worry about putting too much in, just concentrate on expanding your answers to increase the quantity of information.

## 'Even making my writing as small as possible, I need more space than that provided on the form.'

It may be that you started filling in the form without doing a rough copy first in order to work out the spacing required. If the form you are completing is really inadequate for the answers you think are required, you may have to use a separate sheet of paper but do make sure that you are not being long-winded in your answers. You should try to make your replies as concise and simple as possible otherwise you may lose your reader's attention. It will not look impressive if yours is the only application that keeps needing more space. Try using bullet points instead of full sentences and be rigorous about just highlighting the key points in each answer.

## 'I have filled in all my personal details on the form but cannot complete the question about my personality strengths. It's too hard.'

This is one of the most important questions on the form. Employers may well appoint a candidate on the basis of his or her personality who does not have all the desired experience. You need to spend more time thinking about yourself and the sort of person the organisation is looking for. Use the exercise on page 25 to give you some help and rack your brains to collect all the ideas you can about the sort of person you are. Ask friends and relatives for suggestions – but remind them that you only want to hear *good* comments!

## 'I have finished the rough copy of my form but I am nervous that it may still have mistakes in it, even after I've checked it through.'

It is possible to spend so long poring over the document that it becomes impossible to see how well you have done. Have a rest from it for a while and do something totally different. Then come back to the task. Imagine that you have never seen the document before. Does it look well laid out and inviting to a reader? Is your writing tidy and neatly displayed? Are the main points of the form highlighted clearly but unfussily? Show the draft to friends and ask them to check it, and invite their comments on the way you have completed the answers and the way the form looks as a whole. If they agree it looks fine then settle for that, complete the final version and send it off, secure in the knowledge that you have done your best. Always take a copy of the finished version, or at least keep your rough draft, so you can remember exactly what you put on the form if you are invited to attend an interview.

Once you have sent off the form, try to forget about it until the date by which you will hear if you have been shortlisted.

### Points to remember

- You only get one chance to make a good first impression, so if you are serious about wanting the job, commit yourself to putting in the best application you can.
- Time spent making the form look presentable may give you an advantage when the short-list for interview is being considered.

● Work out exactly what you want to include before creating your final version.

## Dos and don'ts

Do:

● write in capital letters if your form is handwritten;
● spread information out on the page to make it easier to read;
● always check your spelling – errors could put the employer off entirely.

Don't:

● change your normal self-expression – try to write as you would talk;
● worry if your answers don't come easily – writing original material is a creative task that can sometimes be difficult;
● give up if you face obstacles – this may be the right job for you, so keep trying to complete the form before the deadline.

# Guidelines and Examples

## Keeping records

When you have applied for a job, keep a copy of the application that you have sent off. You can file it along with the original advert and any paperwork sent to you by the company about the job. A ring-binder or wallet-style folder is ideal for this. Date your copy of the application form so that you know when you sent it off.

You will need this copy if you are invited for an interview, so you can remember what you said about yourself. Even if this particular application goes no further, you may still be able to update and adapt what you have written on a future application for a similar position elsewhere.

## Follow-up

Some employers inform you on the job details that unsuccessful applicants will not be notified, but otherwise they should let you know the outcome. The reason that sometimes no notification is sent is that sending out many letters costs a lot of money. You will still know if you have been successful or not by whether or not you receive an invitation to the next stage of the selection process.

If you do not hear from the employer and you are expecting a reply, you can always ring up to find out what has happened to your application. Make sure that you allow a realistic period for the employer to process the applications and always be polite and courteous when you call.

You will of course feel edgy and keyed-up when you ring, but the tone and type of words you use can make the difference between creating a good impression and alienating the person on the other end of the line.

'I applied for that factory job. Why haven't I heard from you yet?'

This sounds aggressive and is likely to antagonise whoever picks up the telephone. A better approach would be:

'I wonder if you can help me? I recently sent in an application to work in your company and would like to ask if there is any news about an interview shortlist yet.'

Application forms do go astray sometimes, so checking on your progress in this way will ensure that your form has been properly considered and dealt with.

Employers and managers know that applicants are eager to get an interview and will try to be helpful if you sound pleasant and friendly. Similarly, if you are not offered an interview, you could contact the company to try to get some hints about why you were unsuccessful. This depends on your nerve, but a suggested formula could be:

'Thank you for informing me that I have not been successful in my job application. Would it be possible for someone to give me some brief ideas about improving my approach to future vacancies? I would be very grateful for any help that you can offer.'

This could well encourage a full and positive response which could ensure your success next time around, rather than a cagey, non-committal brush-off. The employee will be doing you a favour if he or she does give you feedback of this kind, so make sure you thank him or her properly. 'This is exactly the kind of work I am looking for, so your comments have been really useful. Thank you very much for your time,' is one polite way of responding.

# Examples

The following examples show different questions frequently asked on application forms and explain how you should approach your answers.

## Please describe your main non-work or non-academic interests and tell us why these give you particular satisfaction.

This question is asking about your hobbies and interests but it will not be enough to give a list here. You will need to say why you pursue these interests and what you do with your time. Ideally, your answer should indicate how these interests add to the contribution you could make to the organisation. For instance:

'I am a member of the Northern Cycling Club and regularly participate in group rides. I believe that non-motorised transport is beneficial for the environment and I act as publicity officer for the Club to encourage more cycle-ways in cities and attract more members.'

'I have played and watched football for the last twenty years. I attend my local team's matches whenever possible and coach local youngsters in the season. It is satisfying to help foster talent in other people in this way.'

'I have a talent for baking cakes and make elaborate ones for friends and family when there is a special occasion. I won a prize for an Easter cake last year and was featured in the local paper as a result.'

'I read modern novels as a way of relaxing after work. I have recently tried to do some writing myself and joined a creative writing course to learn the right way to approach the subject.'

## What has been your greatest achievement to date?

You must choose what to answer for yourself here, but think why the employer is asking this question. He or she will make a judgement not so much about the example you give, but about why you think of it as an achievement.

Some ways of answering could include:

'Bringing up my family has to be my greatest achievement. I am proud of the fact that I have good relationships with all three children now they are older and I always make it my first priority to keep a good atmosphere.'

This tells the employer that the candidate is likely to be a helpful person to have around the office – someone who can perhaps stop team conflict before it arises.

'At school I studied a vocational course in the sixth form. Part of the course involved a study of a local factory and I found that I learnt a lot. At the end of the work I had to give a presentation to the whole year group. Despite feeling sick with nerves before I went on, I did my best and now will not feel so shy if I have to talk to a big group again. I learnt that doing plenty of preparation helps you to feel more confident about managing the task.'

This indicates a completely different approach from a younger applicant, and shows that the candidate was determined and quick to learn from the experience.

'I went trekking in the Himalaya mountains during my gap year. It was a terrifying prospect and yet turned out to be an exhilarating experience. I did not think I could cope with the journey at one stage, but the thing that pulled me through was the terrific team work from the group who went. We looked after each other, helped each other to exceed our initial expectations, and are all still firm friends nearly five years later.'

This applicant has an unusual achievement to describe, but its significance is the strength of a good team in problem solving and supporting its members. This understanding will be of use in any workplace, and indicates the writer will be keen to play a full part in any group activities.

'I have been a voluntary trustee of a local charity for the last three years, after the chair asked me to join to help with fundraising. It has been a varied experience with several difficult periods when our funding nearly ran out. I enjoy keeping the staff morale as positive as possible and using my skills to bring more money in for a good cause. I am proud to have kept up my involvement even though volunteering on top of a day job is never easy. I know I help to keep the organisation going.'

This answer demonstrates several things. The candidate is someone who will maintain her effort even when the going gets tough, is motivated by helping others, and will be the person who will give extra effort for the stated aims of the organisation. She sounds like a valuable person to have around at work.

## Please give your reasons for applying for this post.

This question gives you every opportunity to craft a relevant, comprehensive and inspiring picture of what you believe you can contribute to the job. The way that you answer this question depends on the sort of position applied for but here are some examples:

'I am applying for this post because I am a skilled technician and believe that I have a lot to contribute to the job. In my present role I work closely with the pharmacist on duty and make sure that the supplies of drugs and medicines are clearly and safely displayed. I am a hard-working member of the team and can cope with an uneven pressure of work. I communicate well with my superiors and colleagues at all times. I enjoy this work very much and would relish the opportunity to contribute to the work of the General Hospital.'

This candidate makes a clear case for the contribution he can make, explaining the significance of his personality to doing the job very well.

'I have worked in the retail sector for the last five years and am keen to move into a managerial position. I have been on a first-level supervisors course and found it very helpful. I stand in for my manager when he is away and have found the team respond to me very well. I always consult them before taking major decisions, and they know that I will be fair but firm in the way I manage. I enjoy motivating others to work better and find it easy to help sort out any misunderstandings between people.'

This applicant makes the most of her limited supervisory experience to show that she could deal with the major aspects of a management job, dealing with people, decision making and motivating her staff.

'The organisation is moving into a very exciting period with the transition to the new structure. The power to inspect the private sector as well as the public will ensure that patients receive high quality treatment wherever that treatment is located. I am particularly keen to come and join the team now as it has recently begun reviewing ambulance services. One of my responsibilities as a junior reporter was to maintain contact with my local ambulance station, and I feel I could bring some valuable insights to your reports into this areas as a result.'

This applicant is making links between his recent work experience and the position to show how he has special skills that make his application stand out. He is demonstrating that he has something that the other candidates do not, to ensure that he is called for an interview.

## What do you think you would like/dislike most about this job?

When answering this type of question be careful that you do not labour on about the problems to be encountered. Employers want to know that potential candidates are keen and enthusiastic, so a long list of how enjoyable you would find the work will help here. It is fine to be aware of potential difficulties with a job as long as you present them as challenges to be overcome rather than insurmountable obstacles.

Spend some time considering all aspects of the job, looking carefully at any information you have been sent about the post. This question gives you a chance to show that you are clear about the range of responsibility you will face. Just make sure you are positive about the opportunities available if you get this job.

## Is there anything about your health record that you feel we should know?

This type of question is often asked when good health is a requirement of the job. You must use your common sense about the extent to which you reveal your medical history, but if any past illnesses are completely recovered from or would have no effect on your ability to do the job, they need not be mentioned. Be aware that if you do discuss some medical problem on the form, the employer will take it into account when considering your application, so the onus is on you to reassure him or her that you could do the job perfectly well, if this is the case.

## Any question relating to time not accounted for, including unemployment.

This type of question is looking for evidence that you have spent your time profitably. Even if you have been out of work for a long spell, you should be able to show that you have picked up new skills, or perhaps travelled or done some voluntary work while looking for a job.

'I was made redundant from my last job after a major reorganisation process. I took the chance to get involved with a local volunteer scheme clearing out a disused play-space. We gained lottery money so that we could redesign and re-equip the area for local youngsters. The project finished last month and the play area is now in full use. It was launched by the local MP and the event was highlighted in the papers. I learnt a lot about how to get local initiatives up and running, and am now involved in a committee to reclaim more spaces in our area.'

Here is an example of a completed application form for a local authority position. It shows the different sections which normally appear.

From the information given so far, you will see that there are some important basic rules to follow when making applications.

**APPLICATION FORM**

Thank you for your interest - the following information is necessary to ensure that full consideration can be given to all candidates. Whilst the information is confidential, it will be necessary for a small number of authorised staff to have access to it during the selection process. To make copying easier it would be helpful if you would use black ink or type your replies.

Job applied for — ADMINISTRATIVE OFFICER

Department — Social Services

Reference number — SS 2384

Closing date — 08.08.03

Please return this form to — Personnel Section, Social Services Department,

Where did you see the job advertised ?

THE LONDON ECHO NEWSPAPER

**Personal Details**

1  Last name   BISHOP
2  First names   LESLEY
3  Preferred title (eg. Mr, Mrs, Miss, Ms)   MISS
4  Date of birth   4 - 9 - 60
5  Home address   59 LITTLEACRE ROW
   LONDON
   E14 9TN

Telephone   Home  0000-000-0000
Please include the code.

Office  0000-000-0000

May we contact you at work?   Yes ☑ No ☐

**6**  Employment Record (present or most recent employer first)

| Employer's name and address | Job title and main duties | Dates employed and reason for leaving | Salary /Benefits/ Grade where appropriate (Proof may be required) |
|---|---|---|---|
| BAILEY'S GENERAL STORE HIGH STREET LONDON E14 | ADMINISTRATOR : LOOKING AFTER ALL THE PAPERWORK AND WAGES FOR STAFF, DEALING WITH ACCOUNTS ENQUIRIES BY LETTER AND TELE-PHONE, FILING AND WRITING LETTERS, PAYING INVOICES | AUGUST 1985 TO DATE I WOULD LIKE TO WORK IN A LARGER ORGANISATION | £19,000 PA. |
| STEADFAST INSURANCE COMPANY MAIN ROAD SIDCUP, KENT | ADMINISTRATIVE ASSISTANT : HELPING OUT IN THE OFFICE, FILING AND SORTING DOCUMENTS, PROCESSING CLAIMS, ANSWERING THE TELEPHONE ENQUIRIES DUTY, ARRANGING MEETINGS AND TAKING AND TYPING MINUTES | APRIL 1981 TO AUGUST 1985 I WAS OFFERED A MORE RESPONSIBLE JOB ELSEWHERE | £8,000 p.a. |
| BERYL'S FASHION STORE, THE PARADE, LONDON E1 | SALES ASSISTANT: HELPING CUSTOMERS, ORDERING STOCK FROM HEAD OFFICE, KEEPING SHOP CLEAN AND TIDY, WINDOW DISPLAY, CASHING-UP TILL AND HANDLING MONEY, BANKING TAKINGS EACH DAY, PAPERWORK. | MARCH 1978 TO MARCH 1981 | £7,000 PA. |

**7**  Please give details of any voluntary or community work you have been involved with or any outside activities relevant to the post applied for.

I LIKE HELPING OTHER PEOPLE AND DO SHOPPING FOR ELDERLY PEOPLE ON MY ESTATE. THEY ALSO OFTEN ASK ME TO SEE TO THEIR PAPERWORK AND BILLS FOR THEM. I ENJOY HELPING THEM TO KEEP THEIR AFFAIRS IN ORDER.
I ALSO HELP TO RAISE MONEY EACH YEAR FOR A LOCAL HOSPICE. I ORGANISE FUNDRAISING EVENTS WITH A COMMITTEE OF PEOPLE AND TAKE PART MYSELF IN THE DIFFERENT ACTIVITIES. LAST YEAR WE RAISED £5,500 FOR NEW EQUIPMENT.

**8** Secondary and Higher Education / Courses attended

| Dates | Examinations passed and professional qualifications obtained with grades and dates including current studies if any. | Grades |
|---|---|---|
| 1972 – 1977 | HILLTOPS SECONDARY SCHOOL, WANSTEAD ROAD LONDON SE16. <br><br> O'LEVELS IN ENGLISH AND BIOLOGY <br> CSE IN MATHS AND HOME ECONOMICS | C, C <br> 1, 2 |
| 1981 – 1983 | EVENING CLASSES IN BASIC BOOKKEEPING AT SIDCUP ADULT EDUCATION INSTITUTE, LONGSTREET SIDCUP. | PASSED ALL EXAMS |

**9** The Council wishes to encourage people with disabilities to apply for jobs - all information will be treated in confidence.

(i) Do you have a disability?   Yes ☐  No ☑

(ii) If yes, are you currently registered as disabled?   Yes ☐  No ☐

What is the nature of your disability?

N/A

(iii) Do you require special facilities or assistance at the interview or with any aspects of the job if appointed?   Yes ☐  No ☑
If yes please give details on a separate sheet.

**10** If you are applying for job sharing do you have a job share partner?   Yes ☐  No ☐
If yes, please give their name and address.

N/A

**11** Do you require a work permit?   Yes ☐  No ☑

**12** Notice required by present employer _____ ONE MONTH

**13** Are there any dates when you will not be available for interview?

No

**14** Do you hold a full current driving licence?   Yes ☑  No ☐

**15** Are you related to any Councillor or senior officer of the Council?   Yes ☐  No ☑
If yes give details

**Warning** - Canvassing of or failing to disclose relationship to a Councillor may disqualify the candidate.

**16** Those invited for interview may be required to answer formal questions as to whether or not they have unspent convictions or criminal charges or summonses pending against them. Certain posts, eg in Social Services or the Education Department, are exempt from the provisions of the Rehabilitation of Offenders Act 1974. Some posts are subject to political restrictions. If any of the above apply to the post you are applying for, further details will be made available to you.

**17** Please add below details of any special skills, experience or qualifications which make you particularly suited for this job. (An additional sheet may be added if necessary.)

> I ENJOYED SUBJECTS AT SCHOOL WHICH INVOLVED WRITTEN WORK AND WHEN I GOT MY FIRST OFFICE JOB, I WENT TO NIGHT-SCHOOL TO STUDY BOOK-KEEPING. I TOOK TO THIS SUBJECT QUICKLY AND PASSED MY EXAMS, COMING TOP OF THE YEAR GROUP FOR DOUBLE-ENTRY WORK. AT THE INSURANCE COMPANY I LEARNT HOW TO KEEP A BUSY OFFICE WORKING SMOOTHLY AND I FOUND HELPING TO SORT OUT CLIENTS' PROBLEMS WAS VERY SATISFYING. I WAS ASKED TO RUN THE ACCOUNTS OFFICE AT BAILEY'S STORE AND TOOK RESPONSIBILITY FOR ALL THE FINANCIAL DEALINGS OF THIS COMPANY. I AM A MATURE, CALM INDIVIDUAL WHO RESPECTS OTHER PEOPLE AND CAN HELP TO GET THE BEST FROM A STAFF TEAM. I WORK WELL UNDER PRESSURE AND ALWAYS KEEP TO DEADLINES. I HAVE HIGH STANDARDS AND PREFER TO WORK IN A SMALL TEAM OF COLLEAGUES. I AM AN ACCURATE TYPIST, AND CAN BE RELIED UPON TO TAKE RESPONSIBILITY WHEN THE OCCASION ARISES. I AM ESSENTIALLY OF A HAPPY DISPOSITION AND ENJOY BEING FULLY OCCUPIED AT WORK

**18** Please give the name and address of two referees (other than relatives), both of whom should if possible be previous employers, including your present or most recent employer. If school/college leaver please give the name and address of head teacher/tutor. Internal applicants should give the name and extension of their section head.

i) MR MATTHEW BELTON
69 UNDERDOWN LANE
FROGHAMPTON
HAMPSHIRE
SO42 1TT

ii) MRS JUNE BAILEY (OWNER)
℅ BAILEY'S GENERAL STORE
HIGH STREET
LONDON
E14 7TT

> If shortlisted, references may be taken up prior to interview. If you do not want us to approach your present employer at this stage please tick box.  ☑

If you were known by another name when employed please specify: ____—____

**19** I declare that the particulars set out in this application are true in all respects.

Signed _Lesley Breuof_          Date __28-7-03__

## *Points to remember*

- You want the employer to feel that everything in your life so far has been leading up to this point, and that there is no better person for the job than you.
- Try to use every question that is on the form to sell yourself to the employer.
- Spend time thinking about the key areas of work in the job, then establish the skills and experience you have that give you the edge.
- Treat all the sections of the form as equally important. Mess up the early questions and an employer may not bother reading any further.

# Dos and dont's

Do:

- allow yourself plenty of time to complete the form. A rushed application may lose you the job and copies sent by fax never create such a good impression. If you really have to fax a form, make sure you ring the company first to check this is acceptable. Then send the form by post afterwards;
- read the form through carefully first and then follow all the instructions. Plan your answers before you write anything;
- write out your application in rough first. The more care you take over the task, the better your chances of success;
- stress your good points. Let the employer know that he or she would be lucky to have you as an employee;
- make clear and concise points when you write. Waffle is not impressive but personal examples to back up your claims will do the trick.

Don't:

- send in your form after the closing date. It is unlikely to be considered unless you have gained the employer's permission in advance;
- scribble out mistakes. Use correction fluid or put one neat line through the material concerned using a ruler;
- send in your CV with an application form unless you are asked to do so;
- miss out any questions. Check the completed form thoroughly before you send it off. Boxes left blank can give an impression of off-handedness. Remember to sign and date the form if asked to do so. Many people leave this to the end and then forget all about it;
- tell lies. You could lose your job if you are found out.

# 6

# *Letters of Application*

Some job advertisements ask you to send in your CV (curriculum vitae) together with a letter of application. Read *Preparing Your Own CV* (see page viii) to find out how to put together a CV of which you can be proud. Sending a CV to a company with no letter of explanation is confusing, so you need to write a bold, confident and clear letter to accompany it. The letter should be addressed to the named person if you are replying to an advertisement, and it is often helpful to say where you saw the vacancy advertised.

If you are sending the letter as a speculative approach, just to see if the organisation has any vacancies, try to find out the name of the right person to contact and address the letter to him or her personally.

The letter needs to explain the following:

- why you are sending your CV
- significant things about your background and skills
- the sort of person you are
- the special contribution you can offer
- what you would like to happen next
- how you can be contacted.

Everyone who applies for jobs in this way sends in a dynamic letter with their CV, so yours must be strong in order to compete. The letter cannot just be a brief note to say why the CV has arrived; it must be the selling point of the application. As well as details about you and your background, this letter gives you the chance to explain what extra value you can bring to the organisation. This may mean explaining your 'vision' for the position you are applying for – how you would approach the job. Do not make it longer than two sides, and the tone should be courteous and detailed. Do not worry about repeating information contained in your CV. The letter may well be separated from the CV and, in any case, it does no harm to re-state your good points.

You should use good quality paper and word-processed or typed documents are now the norm rather than handwriting. However neat your writing, it is not the same as the employer's and is therefore not nearly as easy to read as typed script. Prove this for yourself by seeing how much faster it is to read newsprint than a letter from someone you do not know. If there is no way you can get access to a method of typing your letter, then work hard to ensure your writing is exceptionally neat and clear.

# Examples

The following pages contain five examples of letters of application for people in different situations. One or more of them may be relevant to you, as you consider how to compose your own letters to employers.

These examples are included to give you an idea of the many different ways in which such letters can be written. Although the names and addresses are fictitious, all the details come from letters written by successful job-seekers. No letter will be appropriate for every situation, but the examples have been chosen to represent a range of circumstances. Do not copy these letters, but see if they give you ideas for approaches of your own.

# 1 Speculative approach

Maria MacDonald
Basement Flat
2 Arbour Fields
Richmond
N Yorks

15 April 2003

Mr David Belton
Director
Salcott Equipment
33 Pinks Lane
Richmond
N Yorks

Dear Mr Belton

I am writing to enquire if you have any vacancies in your company. I enclose my CV for your information. As you can see, I have spent ten years working with a variety of different machinery and equipment and am used to industrial work.

I am a steady and serious person who works hard and fits easily into a new team. I am clean and careful in my work and can lend a hand in the office when needed. I am quick to pick up new instructions and flexible about the hours that I work. It was normal for me to do shift-work in my last job. I am known for taking a pride in my work and want to work for a company with a reputation for producing quality goods – hence my application to Salcott's.

I have excellent references and would be delighted to discuss any possible vacancy with you at your convenience. In case you do not have any suitable openings at the moment, I would be grateful if you would keep my CV on file for any future possibilities.

Thank you for your attention to this matter. I look forward to hearing from you.

Yours sincerely

Maria MacDonald

Enc:

## 2    College leaver

Adrian Miller
97 Potter's Close
Sedgefield
Teesside
RT3 3PP

24 October 2003

Ms Louise Powell
Powell's Energy Company
200 Seymour Industrial Estate
Hartfield Road
Middlesbrough GT99 1LZ

Dear Ms Powell

Please find enclosed my CV in application for the post advertised in the *Guardian* on 20 October.

The nature of my degree course has prepared me for this position. The course involved a great deal of independent research, relying on a substantial amount of translating into French and Spanish. I also studied economic history and for one course (History of Latin America since Independence) an understanding of the petro-chemical industry was essential. I found this subject very stimulating.

I am a fast and accurate writer, with a keen eye for detail and I should be very grateful for the opportunity to progress to market reporting.

I have not only the ability to take on the responsibility of this position immediately, but I believe that I also have the enthusiasm and determination to ensure that I make a success of it.

Thank you for taking the time to consider this application and I look forward to hearing from you in the near future.

Yours sincerely


Adrian Miller

Enc:

# 3    Woman returner

Sherena Williams
Hazelwood Cottage
Sandy Hill
Sway
Hampshire

12 December 2003

The Personnel Manager
Hall's Ltd
100 London Road
Brockenhurst
Hampshire

Dear Sir/Madam

Re: Accounts Manager Vacancy

I am writing in reply to your advertisement in this week's *Hampshire Times*. I enclose my CV for your information. As you can see, I trained in accounting at Bishop's Technical College gaining a BTEC pass in 1982. For the next ten years I ran the accounts department of Nicholson's Bakery in Lymington. I covered the whole variety of work in this busy office, from handling petty cash and making wage payments to credit control. I regularly used computerised accounts packages.

I left this post in 1992 to bring up my two young children. Being a full-time parent has enabled me to acquire new skills, such as scheduling and keeping to deadlines, organising, communicating on different levels, delegating work and using my creative imagination to solve problems.

I am patient and flexible, stay calm in difficult situations, and am confident when working with figures and running an office. I am hard-working and thorough and am looking forward to resuming my career with a pace-making organisation like Hall's.

I would be happy to discuss this application in more detail and look forward to hearing from you.

Yours faithfully

Sherena Williams

Enc:

# 4　School/College leaver

Fola Okintola
111 Poulton Terrace
Sidcup
Kent

1 September 2003

The Personnel Director
Haddleston Council
Haddleston
Kent

Dear Sir/Madam

Re: Vacancies for Junior Trainees

I would like to apply for the vacancy for junior trainee which I saw in my local careers office.

I left Cole Comprehensive School this year after taking my GCSE exams. I passed in English, Mathematics and General Science and won a prize for a project on 'Science and Ecology' earlier in my final year. I enclose a copy of my CV and my Record of Achievement which shows my progress throughout the last two years.

I am good at bringing the best out of other people and spent my sports lessons at school being a key player in the volleyball team. I have worked each summer for the last three years as an assistant in the local sports centre helping to organise the summer sports programme which the Council runs each year for school children.

I am interested in working for the Council because I believe that local services are important. I take a pride in living in this area and know that your recent Quality Initiative has made people realise how much they depend on good street lighting and cleaning, housing and leisure facilities.

I would like to become a part of the team of people that organises such services and look forward to discussing how I can contribute to the work of the Council in due course.

Thank you for your time. I look forward to hearing from you.

Yours faithfully

Fola Okintola

Enc:

# 5   Mature candidate

Louis Coombe
80 Bryan Ridge
Westminster Parade
London SW15

14 February 2003

Mrs Alberga
Personnel Manager
Kogan and Company
Norman Street
London W1

Dear Mrs Alberga

Re: Adviser, Training Unit

Please find enclosed my CV. I have had many years' successful experience as a personnel manager in the clothing industry. Working with teams of different people meant that I quickly became adaptable and flexible.

I am at present updating my computer skills at a local resource centre and I have been helping the tutors there, on a voluntary basis, with the new trainees. I introduce them to the centre and act as a mentor during their training programme.

I devote time to making sure that everyone works well together and can recognise problems before they become insurmountable. I am approachable and tolerant but maintain high standards and the ability to communicate quickly and clearly with others. I am known for my ability to make learning fun and can always motivate people to give more of themselves. My mature outlook allows me to be a soothing influence at difficult times and I have a wide experience of work to draw on when needed.

I would enjoy contributing to the training provided by your company as I know of your excellent reputation in this field. I have a relative who works in your Northern Region who tells me that your staff development programme is very good.

I would be delighted to discuss any detail of my application at your convenience. Thank you for your attention to this matter. I look forward to hearing from you.

Yours sincerely

Louis Coombe

Enc:

Notice how in each of these examples the candidates are trying to phrase their application in terms that will appeal to the employer. They have thought through:

- what the job involves
- what they have to offer in skills and experience that can be transferred to the new position
- how their personalities will fit.

They have made sure that they convey this clearly and simply in their letters. They sound keen without giving the impression that they are desperate. Most important, they spend time demonstrating to the reader how they can contribute to the organisation.

Notice also how they write the letter itself. They know that their letter must be easy to read and follow if they are to attract the employer's attention when he or she has a pile of other applications to consider. They write as if they were sitting and talking in front of the employer at an interview – clearly but politely. Good writing does not mean using the longest words and the most complicated sentences that you can think up. It means being concise and to the point, and keeping your sentences short.

None of the letters is gimmicky or flashy. All the writers believe that they have serious skills to offer and the right personalities to fit into the environment concerned. Their letters convey that information to the employer in an impressive way. You can tell that each writer has spent time and trouble composing the letter in order to make sure that it hits the mark.

Each letter ends with a thank you and is correctly addressed and typed for easy reading.

# Letters with your application form

Some employers expect a brief letter to accompany the application form. These are the views of the Director of Communications for a health organisation that regularly recruits office staff:

'Do send a covering letter but don't make it too long. It is not like sending a CV where the letter is part of the application but it still needs to be more than "Please find my application enclosed. I look forward to expanding on this at interview." I always read the covering letter as I find it helps me form a first impression and differentiates between the different applications I am seeing. I expect you to give me one paragraph about why you are great for the job and why you would like to come and work for me.'

## Points to remember

- Letters of application can echo the key points from your application or CV, but should state your reasons for applying in different words.
- You can use a letter to bring out factors that are particularly relevant to the post, particularly if you are sending it with an application form where your answers may have been more constrained by the questions on the form.
- Tailor and rewrite each letter for the specific job you are applying for. Cutting and pasting big chunks of typing from previous applications looks clumsy and will not impress.

## Dos and don'ts

Do:

- limit the letter to only two sides of A4 at most;
- give examples of the claims you are making for yourself;
- keep sentences short and punchy if you want the letter to be read.

Don't:

- talk about why you want the job: the employer is only interested in what you have to offer;
- sound dull: use enthusiastic language to show you are keen;
- close any doors. Try to get your letter and CV kept on file if there turn out to be no current vacancies.

# 7

# How to Get That Job!

## Case studies

All the characters in the following case studies had some difficulty with their application forms. Read their stories to illustrate what can go wrong and to see how they could improve their techniques.

### Wayne

Wayne was quite good at filling in application forms and was always keen to do his extensive experience justice. He had some trouble fitting in details of all his varied jobs in the 'Previous Experience' space provided, despite keeping his writing small and neat. He added an extra piece of paper to ensure that everything was included.

The employer said:

'It is ridiculous to cram in so much tiny writing in order to get all your jobs included. It put me off trying to read through it, especially as a lot of them had nothing in common with the post I am trying to fill. He would have done himself much more favour if he had just highlighted those jobs that were particularly relevant to this position. He could then have indicated that he also had other experience to offer, but just summarised what that was rather than listing each position. The whole experience was depressing, as an otherwise good candidate made himself appear a bad judge of how to present himself on the form.'

## Mark

Mark prided himself on having excellent writing skills. He dashed off his applications with a flourish and was confident that the content of his forms was always excellent. He had worked in senior positions in the past and knew he had a lot to offer. He never bothered to do a rough copy first because he was an experienced job applicant and felt it would just be a waste of his time.

The employer said:

'Mark's form was just messy. He could have been quite an impressive candidate but the application looks as though he had taken no time over its completion. The way he presented himself put me off spending any more time on this form. Candidates have to understand that with many, many forms (sometimes up to 100) in front of me, I am not going to bother digging out nuggets. Unless everything about an application is impressive, it goes on the reject pile, I'm afraid.'

## Leila

Leila really wanted the job and her employer had asked her to put in for the promotion position. She was thrilled to have been encouraged to apply, and gave herself several weeks to fill the form in. Every evening after work she sat down and tried to complete it, but found she could just not get started. She got more and more worried as the deadline approached and there was still nothing written on her rough copy. The last night she rushed to fill in the form, but by the time it was finished, she was so disappointed in the way it looked, she tore it up and put it in the bin.

The employer said:

'We were so keen for Leila to apply for the job and had specifically suggested to her that she did so. For some reason she missed the dead-line and did not put an application in at all. For the lack of that form, she missed her chance for a significant promotion and seven thousand more pounds a year. To be honest, a terribly presented form that just listed her present responsibilities would have got her an interview, because the promotion was right up her street. Without the application form there was nothing we could do but give the job to the next best candidate.'

## Victoria

Victoria tried very hard with her application form. She felt she would be good at the job concerned but she was also worried about how to sell herself on paper. She spent weeks fretting over the form, asking friends to comment on what she had written and rewriting it several times. She was concerned that she show herself to be an honest person who did not make any claims about her abilities that could not be sub-stantiated.

The employer said:

'This form was just boring compared to all the others. She seemed to not really want the job. Most applicants come over as keen to state their strong points, but Victoria was so low-key that it was hard to find any particular contribution that she thought she could make. Application forms have to work extra hard to make the candidate sound dynamic and significant, otherwise we have no reason to invite them to come and tell us more at interview.'

## Stephen

Stephen knew he could do the job on offer. He had not long left college and the vacancy was perfect for his skills and person-ality. The trouble was that he did not have any very relevant experience. He filled in the form as best he could, stating his claim that he would be very good in the position and was keen to get to the interview stage so that he could impress them with his character and outlook.

The employer said:

'Unfortunately we could not take the risk of bringing Stephen in to the interview phase of this recruitment exercise. He may have been a great candidate but he did not make a good enough case for his inclusion on his application form. Without any relevant experience since college, we had nothing to go on to take this application further. He said he thought he would be good but gave no examples to illustrate why this was the case. If he had made some links with college activities to the work we do, or if he could have shown how he had picked up his understanding of our work, it may have been different. If your form does not shout loudly that you should be kept in, then you will be out. A bit more thought about how much needs to go in to the form could have saved the day.'

# Step-by-step checklist

## Step 1.  Planning

When you receive your application form take a copy and put the original away safely until you are ready to write up the final version. Now read your copy through carefully. Re-read the job advertisement and any other details of the job or company that you may have, including the job description and personnel specification. These documents will tell you exactly how the employer will rate you for your suitability for the position. You may wish to do some other research into the business or the type of work involved. At the very least, look up the organisation on the Internet and see if there is a company Web site to give you additional information.

A *job description*, as its name suggests, describes the main activities in the job. It lists, often in order of importance, the work that the successful candidate will be doing. You need to use this document to show how you could cope with the job.

Do not just state that you are capable of everything that is asked for, but rather give brief examples to illustrate what you have achieved in these areas previously.

A *personnel specification* is a list prepared by employers in relation to a particular job, to describe the type of person that they are looking for. It details the character traits that they would like and those particular skills or experience that may be ESSENTIAL or PREFERRED for the post.

If a personnel specification is included with the details sent to you about a job, it is not there just for guidance in filling out the form. You must show that you possess any ESSENTIAL skills or qualities asked for. Your application will be more favourably considered if you can also demonstrate that you have those PREFERRED for the work. A simple assertion that you have the skill required will not do. You need to take each requirement in turn and think of an example which shows your ability in this area.

Spend time thinking about the sort of person you are, recap your employment history, mulling over the things that you have done particularly well in the past, and any praise that you received in the work environment or in a personal capacity. Take stock of your CV and think of work-related examples which will prove to an employer that you would be good at the job advertised. Boost your confidence as much as possible so that you will not hold back once you start filling in your application. Most candidates fail at this stage because they do not present their good points and strengths adequately.

## Step 2.  Preparation

Now you are ready to do some serious work to tie up what the employer is looking for with your experience. Spend some time thinking over the details of the job. You can use your common sense to work out what sort of person the employer is looking for. Does he or she need any specific skills or experience?

Underline all the key points from the original advertisement, job description and personnel specification.

Remember that you can describe the same job in different ways. For example, in one case you may emphasise the experience you gained in handling projects and achieving targets through communicating with people. In another case you may need to emphasise the amount of work you did, analysing and interpreting data, preparing reports and contributing to the development of new ideas, policies and procedures. Draft your answers on your copy and make sure that you respond to all the questions and fill up all the available space. It has been provided for that purpose and half-empty boxes will not be sufficient.

Remember that the employer is also interested in your personality. Make sure that you analyse your strengths and personal characteristics so that you can demonstrate your suitability for the job. Job applicants tend to spend a great deal of time writing about their skills and experience and expend too little effort in trying to convey their character traits, when the latter may be the most important factor to the employer.

Think back through your work experience, whether paid or voluntary, and choose examples which tie in with the work involved in this job to show how you would be a good employee. Put your answers down on the page. You may need to make two or three attempts before you feel happy with your answer, particularly with the difficult questions such as: 'What skills and experience do you have that make you particularly suitable for this job?' These questions are meant to test you, to see if you can provide well thought-out and appropriate answers, so take them seriously.

Take plenty of time at this stage. As a general rule, the number of days that you work on this form from start to finish should equal the number of pages of the form.

Get a friend or relative to check over the rough copy of the form for you. They may spot missed questions or spelling mistakes that you have not noticed, and can see if your answers make sense.

## Step 3.  Putting it all together

Once you are satisfied with your answers, you can transfer your work on to the final copy of the form. Take great care – this must be as neat as you can possibly make it. You will be judged mainly on the way that you present yourself on paper, and no matter how excellent your answers, if the form looks messy you are unlikely to be chosen for interview. Take pride in the application and enjoy the challenge of showing off your attributes and talents. Again, at this stage, get someone to look at the form for you. Silly mistakes are easy to miss when you have been buried in the same form for ages. Have you remembered to sign it at the bottom if asked to do so? Keep a copy of the finished version that you send off, and put the date on it, so that you have a neat record of what the employer will see.

## Step 4.  Follow-up

You need to be systematic about your job-hunting. When you send off your completed form, keep a copy for your records (just in case you are called for interview) and store the copy together with the original advert and any other information that you may have about the job. Perhaps all these pieces of paper could be put in a special file, dated, and kept tidily in case you need to refer to them again. You may apply for a similar job in the future, and you can save yourself some work if you have already thought out your answers.

Unless the employer has told you that you will only be notified if you are shortlisted for the vacancy, you should expect to hear from the company after the closing date. It does not hurt to get in touch with the employer if you are not contacted. A friendly enquiry, something like: 'I applied for a vacancy with your company recently but have not heard from you yet. I wonder if I could ask if there is any news?' may answer your question. Remember not to sound aggressive on the telephone. 'I applied for a job with you two weeks ago. Why haven't you called me for interview?' will probably not encourage a positive reply.

The point of following up vacancies in this way is twofold. First, there is always the possibility that your application may have been mislaid or forgotten and your call may help to sort out the problem. Second, even if you have not been successful you could ask the employer for tips to help you improve future attempts.

Handling rejection is not easy for any of us and yet we all need to be able to keep moving forward. Even the most successful people get turned down sometimes. Resist the inclination to think that there is something wrong with you if you are rejected for a job. If you genuinely feel that you worked hard on your application and represented your experience, skills and personality as best you could, you should congratulate yourself. If the employer had the chance to get to know you through your form, perhaps you were not quite suitable for the vacancy compared to other candidates. The reason why you did not succeed can only be guessed at, but it is likely that there just happened to be someone with more appropriate experience than you on the day.

Your turn will soon come as long as you keep your standards of presentation as high as possible. The chances are that there is an even better job just round the corner. You can take comfort from the fact that all the work you put in on your application may come in useful for a similar vacancy in the future, with some minor alterations to gear it up to the next job.

The best antidote to feeling demoralised is to keep on applying for other jobs. If possible, each time you are waiting to hear about one job, send off an application for another so that you always have one to look forward to. Sometimes it is a disheartening experience to feel that you are not succeeding with your job search. You need to keep your confidence high by feeling a sense of achievement in some other area of your life. Participate in some voluntary work, where your abilities will be appreciated while you wait to get a job, or learn a new skill to improve your chances of being shortlisted for interview.

Try to keep learning about yourself: how you come over to others, what you are good at and what skills you can develop. And learn about others: what makes them successful and impressive? With this attitude, even the longest period of not getting the job you want can be turned into an advantageous learning experience.

Above all, keep believing that you are special, that you have a lot to offer and that you will eventually arrive at where you want to be. As soon as you are in a satisfying job, this period of making applications, which seems to be dragging on, will be hard to recall. If you are reading this book without any particular job to apply for at the moment, remember to re-read it when you have your next important form to complete. Good luck!

## Points to remember

- Even the most employable and brilliant candidates get rejected sometimes, so do not let a disappointment get you down.
- Application forms can seem the least exciting part of the recruitment process, but they represent the gateway to the all-important interview.
- Completing an application form you feel proud of can be an excellent rehearsal for meeting the employer in person later on.
- Without the time to think through why you would make a good contribution to the post, you would be unconfident at the interview.

- You know if the employer takes your application further that there is no reason why you should not get the job.

## Dos and don'ts

Do:

- change your approach if you keep getting rejected at the application stage;
- involve other people you trust in your efforts: sometimes a different point of view can help you complete the more difficult questions when you get stuck;
- keep the rest of your life going while you are applying for jobs: you need to remain a well-rounded person, not turn into a job search bore.

Don't:

- tell the world about every job you apply for – it can be embarrassing if you don't get anywhere;
- get overwhelmed by the task ahead: everyone has to complete application forms and we all find it difficult sometimes;
- give up. If you keep making applications and keep trying to improve you will get there one day soon.

# Application form blanks

You may find these blank forms useful to practise on, even if there is no particular job vacancy that you are interested in at the moment. Use the checklist on pages 88–93 to remind you of the best way to complete them.

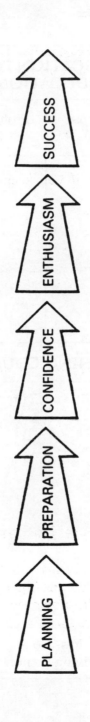

PLANNING → PREPARATION → CONFIDENCE → ENTHUSIASM → SUCCESS

| APPLICATION FORM EDUCATION | | |
|---|---|---|
| Academic Qualifications (please give subjects) | | Professional Qualifications (please give dates) |
| | | |

## TRAINING COURSES

| Organising Body | Title of Course | Dates Attended |
|---|---|---|
| | | |

Are you a car owner?   Yes/No
Do you hold a valid driving licence?   Yes/No

## EMPLOYMENT HISTORY

| Employer (current or most recent first) | Job title and brief description of duties | Grade | Salary | Dates employed | Reason for leaving |
|---|---|---|---|---|---|
| | | | | | |

## ADDITIONAL INFORMATION

Please give the following information:

(A)   The reasons why you are applying for this post.

(B)   Any experience you may have which is related to this post.

## INTERESTS AND ACTIVITIES

Briefly outline your hobbies and interests

Please give the names and addresses of two referees:–
(ONE MUST BE YOUR PRESENT EMPLOYER)

| | |
|---|---|
| NAME ............................................. | NAME ............................................. |
| POSITION ...................................... | POSITION ...................................... |
| ADDRESS ....................................... | ADDRESS ....................................... |
| ....................................................... | ....................................................... |
| ....................................................... | ....................................................... |
| ....................................................... | ....................................................... |
| POSTCODE ..................................... | POSTCODE ..................................... |
| MAY WE CONTACT PRIOR TO INTERVIEW? | MAY WE CONTACT PRIOR TO INTERVIEW? |
| YES/NO | YES/NO |

NOTICE PERIOD REQUIRED?

IF SELECTED FOR INTERVIEW WOULD YOU BE AVAILABLE ON

...........................................?   YES/NO

I confirm that to the best of my knowledge the information given on this form is true and can be treated as any subsequent Contract of Employment.

Date .........................................................    Signature ...........................................

## APPLICATION FORM

For Office Use

APPLICATION FOR THE POST OF _____

PERSONAL DETAILS

FORENAME(S) _____    SURNAME_____

ADDRESS _____

_____

(INCLUDING POST CODE) _____

DATE OF BIRTH _____    SEX: MALE/FEMALE

TELEPHONE: HOME _____    DAYTIME _____

CURRENT DRIVING LICENCE: YES/NO    CAR OWNER: YES/NO

---

Do you have any special requirements to enable you to attend for interview, eg access, interpreters? Please indicate below.

## DETAILS OF EDUCATION, TRAINING AND QUALIFICATIONS

| Dates Attended | Full-time or Part-time | Name and Town of Secondary School/College/ University | Qualifications/ Examinations – state subjects & examining board | Date Gained |
|---|---|---|---|---|
|  |  |  |  |  |

## REFERENCES

Two persons to whom approach may be made should be listed. If you do not wish any reference to be sought at this stage, please place an X in the relevant box.

Name:                                    Name:

Full Address:                        Full Address:

Telephone No:                     Telephone No:

PLEASE INDICATE YOUR REASONS FOR SEEKING THIS POST,
HIGHLIGHTING ANY PERSONAL SKILLS WHICH YOU BELIEVE
WOULD BE OF PARTICULAR RELEVANCE OR VALUE.

PAST EMPLOYMENT    (Please include part-time or holiday jobs)

Employer:                                    Type of Work/Responsibilities

VOLUNTARY WORK EXPERIENCE          (For example, involvement in
                                                                     community fundraising, play
                                                                     group, committee work.)

PRESENT EMPLOYMENT    (if applicable)
Employer's Name            ..............................................................................
and Address                   ..............................................................................
                                       ..............................................................................
Date Started                  ..............................................................................
Type of Work/Responsibilities:

# Confidential application form

Position applied for

How did you hear of the vacancy?

---

Surname (Mr/Mrs/Ms/Miss)            (BLOCK LETTERS PLEASE)
                                    Address

Forenames

Telephone No. (Home)                (Work)

Nationality                         Date of birth

---

Are you prepared to move house –    What locations in England and Wales
                                    would be most and least acceptable to
                                    you?

For this position                   Most acceptable

For future promotion                Least acceptable

---

Do you have a full driving licence?    YES/NO

---

To assist us in monitoring our policy of equal opportunities, we would be grateful if
you could tick the appropriate box.
I would describe my ethnic origin as

| African | Afro-Caribbean | Asian | European–UK | European–other | Other – please specify |
|---------|----------------|-------|-------------|----------------|------------------------|
| ☐ | ☐ | ☐ | ☐ | ☐ | ☐ |

## School Record (after age 11)

| Name & address of School/College | Dates From To | Educational Qualifications (specify all subjects and attempts) | | | | | |
|---|---|---|---|---|---|---|---|
| | | 'O' levels or equivalent | | | | | |
| | | Subject | Grade | Date | Subject | Grade | Date |
| | | | | | | | |
| | | 'A' levels or equivalent | | | | | |
| | | Subject | Grade | Date | Subject | Grade | Date |
| | | | | | | | |

## Further Education Record

| Name of Universities/Colleges attended (f/t or p/t) plus dates | Subjects taken | BSc, BA etc | Qualification Level/Class expected or obtained | Date obtained |
|---|---|---|---|---|
| | | | | |

## Professional Qualifications

| Give the dates and results of all professional examinations taken (including intermediate stages) | Results | Dates |
|---|---|---|
| | | |

# Employment History

Please give details of your present or most recent job

From                                    Main duties and responsibilities

To

Name and address of employer

                                        Main achievements

Nature of business

Job title                               Organisation chart indicating your main position

Starting salary

Most recent salary

Reason for leaving

Please give details of your second most recent job

From                                    Main duties and responsibilities

To

Name and address of employer

                                        Main achievements

Nature of business

Job title                               Organisation chart indicating your main position

Starting salary

Most recent salary

Reason for leaving

Please list any job before those mentioned overleaf

| From | To | Name of employer | Job title | Start | Salary | Finish |
|------|-----|------------------|-----------|-------|--------|--------|

---

## Interests/Responsibilities
What are your main interests/responsibilities outside work?

---

## Career Plans
Describe briefly the development of your career to date, your plans for the future and the attraction of this job.

---

Are there any particular questions you would like to raise at interview?

---

Any further information you may care to give which may be relevant to your application.

---

## Referees

Please give the name, address and position of two referees who can comment on your work performance. At least one of these should be connected with your present (or most recent) place of employment or study.

1.                                        2.

Position                                  Position

Please give the name, address and occupation of one referee unconnected with employment who has known you for at least three years to whom reference may be made.

Occupation

Have you been convicted of any criminal offences which are not yet 'spent' under the Rehabilitation of Offenders Act 1974?
(Please give details or answer 'No')

Please give details of any major illness and/or any chronic conditions/allergies.

Please give details of any time lost from work/full-time education in the last five years through ill health or other incapacity.

Are you registered disabled?   YES/NO

How much notice are you required to give?

Signature                                 Date

Note:   a) It will be accepted that we may approach your past employers (BUT NOT YOUR PRESENT EMPLOYER), unless you make a note to the contrary below, showing the organisation we may not approach without prior permission.
     b) Any false or misleading statements made on this form may, if they subsequently come to light, be taken to justify dismissal from employment with the Commission or could result in the cancellation of any job offer made.

# Using the Internet to Help You with Job Search Activities and Application Forms

There are many sites on the Internet that give you assistance with job search. Most are sites displaying job vacancies. They make their money from recruitment advertising by employers, or by taking a commission from employers if they place you in a job. As part of the information they provide around searching for jobs, these sites often include tips on CVs, completing applications and other career development issues.

Job-seekers can access these pages free of charge, although if you want to use their specialised targeting process for locating the most relevant jobs to suit you, you may be required to go through a registration process. Many sites have an e-mail facility that can let you know regularly about targeted jobs that fit your profile.

The World Wide Web is a fast-changing scene, and new sites appear as fast as others fall from view. Here are 10 of the current best for UK job-seekers.

# 1  www.timesonline.co.uk

The Web site of the *Times* newspaper group. This site contains 'classifieds', their jobs pages. These are particularly useful for senior, managerial, technical and secretarial vacancies. The site also includes topical interview tips and career development articles.

# 2  www.prospects.ac.uk

Labelled as the UK's official graduate careers Web site, this site is provided by the Higher Education Careers Services Unit and the Association of Graduate Careers Advisory Services. It is aimed at graduates and provides 'the essential guide to graduate careers and postgraduate study in the UK' according to the home page.

Accessible and functional, this is a useful resource for graduates, and by gathering all the key points together can help to focus graduate job search or path to further study.

# 3  www.jobs.guardian.co.uk

'The UK's most popular newspaper Web site.' Provided by the *Guardian* newspaper group: the *Guardian* is the national newspaper with the largest selection of jobs. This site is accessible and impressive, and is easy to search for jobs by relevance to your needs. It has many new jobs every day, listed by broad sector and seniority, and is worth checking on a regular basis for national-level jobs.

# 4  www.ft.com

This is the recruitment site provided by the *Financial Times* newspaper. It includes job vacancies, particularly in the financial sector, and some job search tips.

# 5  www.jobs.co.uk

Labelling itself 'The one-stop jobs supersite', this site searches all of the UK jobs boards for you to find vacancies that may suit you. It offers a list of sites that can help with job search, and assesses them for the amount of information they provide, ease of use and so on. This site includes CV and interview advice, and links up direct to all the sites it finds for you.

# 6  www.doctorjob.com

Doctorjob is a careers publisher's Web site, featuring a lot of careers information and graduate employment opportunities displayed in a quirky style with cartoons.

# 7  www.reed.co.uk

This site is owned by Reed Employment, a leading employment agency. It includes voluntary opportunities and career tips, including techniques to improve your applications.

# 8  www.bradleycvs.co.uk

This is a CV service company offering information about job search skills. This site also has many links to other specific recruitment sites.

# 9  www.monster.co.uk

A commercial recruitment Web site with extensive job search advice included.

# 10  www.jobpilot.co.uk

A recruitment Web site with some job search tips included.

# *Sources of Help*

## Service Connexions

Careers officers and personal advisers work with young people and sometimes adults to help them find the job or training of their choice. They may be able to help you by checking over your form and they may provide access to a careers library where you can find information about different employers and jobs. Careers advisers will certainly be able to direct you to local resources for job-seekers. Find the number of your local Connexions Service in the phone book and ring to find out more.

## Libraries

Libraries can be quiet places to complete application forms and the reference sections of main libraries have information about different companies and large employers so you can find out about the main products and services and the company organisation. Ask the librarian for help. Many libraries also have photocopiers for use by the public for a fee and can often provide Internet access too.

# Jobcentres

Government-funded jobcentres have skilled staff who can advise you on the best way to make applications. If you have been unemployed for a while you can use their job search facilities such as telephones, stationery, and sometimes computers to help you get a job. Contact your local Jobcentre for details: their telephone number will be in your local telephone directory.

# Learn Direct

The Learn Direct Helpline (0800 100 900) is funded by the government and gives advice about local sources of help on careers and learning issues. This could include how to contact the organisations mentioned above. If you ask specifically where you can get help with job search skills, they will find out your most suitable local resource.

# *Index*

# Further Reading from Kogan Page

## Other titles in the testing series

*Career, Aptitude and Selection Tests*, Jim Barrett, 1998
*How to Master Personality Questionnaires*, 2nd edn, Mark Parkinson, 2000
*How to Master Psychometric Tests*, 2nd edn, Mark Parkinson, 2000
*How to Pass Advanced Aptitude Tests*, Jim Barrett, 2002
*How to Pass at an Assessment Centre*, Harry Tolley and Bob Wood, 2001
*How to Pass Computer Selection Tests*, Sanjay Modha, 1994
*How to Pass Graduate Psychometric Tests*, 2nd edn, Mike Bryon, 2001
*How to Pass Numeracy Tests*, 2nd edn, Harry Tolley and Ken Thomas, 2000
*How to Pass Professional-level Psychometric Tests*, Sam Al-Jajjoka, 2001
*How to Pass Selection Tests*, 2nd edn, Mike Bryon and Sanjay Modha, 1998
*How to Pass Technical Selection Tests*, Mike Bryon and Sanjay Modha, 1993
*How to Pass the Civil Service Qualifying Tests*, Mike Bryon, 1995
*How to Pass the Police Initial Recruitment Test*, Harry Tolley, Ken Thomas and Catherine Tolley, 1997
*How to Pass Verbal Reasoning Tests*, Harry Tolley and Ken Thomas, 2000
*Rate Yourself!*, Marthe Sansregret and Dyane Adams, 1998
*Test Your IQ*, Ken Russell and Philip Carter, 2000
*Test Your Own Aptitude*, 2nd edn, Jim Barrett and Geoff Williams, 1990
*Test Yourself!*, Jim Barrett, 2000
*The Times Book of IQ Tests – Book One*, Ken Russell and Philip Carter, 2001
*The Times Book of IQ Tests – Book Two*, Ken Russell and Philip Carter, 2002

## Also available on CD ROM in association with *The Times*

Published by Kogan Page Interactive, *The Times* Testing Series is an exciting new range of interactive CD ROMs that will provide invaluable practice tests for both job applicants and for those seeking a brain-stretching challenge. Each CD ROM features:

● over 1000 unique interactive questions;
● instant scoring with feedback and analysis;
● hours of practice with randomly generated test;
● questions devised by top UK MENSA puzzles editors and test experts;
● against-the-clock, real test conditions.

current titles available:
*Brain Teasers Volume 1*, 2002
*Psychometric Tests Volume 1*, 2002
*Test Your IQ Volume 1*, 2002
*Test Your Aptitude Volume 1*, 2002

## Interview and career guidance

*The A–Z of Careers and Jobs*, 10th edn, Irene Krechowiecka, 2002
*Act Your Way Into a New Job*, Deb Gottesman and Buzz Mauro, 1999
*Changing Your Career*, Sally Longson, 2000
*Choosing Your Career*, Simon Kent, 1997
*Creating Your Career*, Simon Kent, 1997
*From CV to Shortlist*, Tony Vickers, 1997
*Graduate Job Hunting Guide*, Mark Parkinson, 2001
*Great Answers to Tough Interview Questions*, 5th edn, Martin John Yate, 2001
*How You Can Get That Job!*, 3rd edn, Rebecca Corfield, 2002
*The Job-Hunter's Handbook*, 2nd edn, David Greenwood, 1999
*Job-Hunting Made Easy*, 3rd edn, John Bramham and David Cox, 1995
*Landing Your First Job*, Andrea Shavick, 1999
*Net That Job!*, 2nd edn, Irene Krechowiecka, 2000
*Odd Jobs*, 2nd edn, Simon Kent, 2002
*Offbeat Careers*, 3rd edn, Vivien Donald, 1995
*Online Job-Hunting: Great Answers to Tough Interview Questions*, Martin John Yate and Terra Dourlain, 2001
*Preparing Your Own CV*, 3rd edn, Rebecca Corfield, 2002
*Readymade CVs*, 2nd edn, Lynn Williams, 2000
*Readymade Job Search Letters*, 2nd edn, Lynn Williams, 2000
*Successful Interview Skills*, 3rd edn, Rebecca Corfield, 2002
*Your Job Search Made Easy*, 3rd edn, Mark Parkinson, 2002

Further advice on a variety of specific career paths can also be found in Kogan Page's *Careers in...* series and *Getting a Top Job in...* series. Please visit the Web site at the address below for more details.

---

The above titles are available from all good bookshops. For further information, please contact the publisher at the following address:

Kogan Page Limited
120 Pentonville Road
London N1 9JN
Tel: 020 7278 0433
Fax: 020 7837 6348
www.kogan-page.co.uk